Preface

The Power of Project Success

In virtually every industry, the dominant companies are those that consistently beat their competition to the punch in the development and launching of new products, technologies, systems, programs, and facilities; those companies that accomplish the most successful mergers and acquisitions; the ones that stage the most effective marketing campaigns and special events.

The ability to perform projects faster, more effectively, and at lower cost than their competition generates competitive advantage for those companies, especially in a business environment characterized by accelerating change. The ability to achieve project success consistently will create competitive advantage for your organization as well.

The power of project success is real, and if you don't yet possess it, you are at a significant disadvantage relative to those who do.

For more than 25 years, my associates at Project Success, Incorporated (formerly YCA) and I have worked with more than 600 client organizations, developing a better way, an easier way, of managing projects successfully. The result of that effort is *The Project Success Method, A Proven Approach to Achieving Superior Project Performance in as Little as 5 Days.*

While an estimated 70 to 90 percent of strategic initiatives fail, companies that employ The Project Success Method consistently plan and control their projects effectively. They execute projects with higher quality, faster, and at lower cost. How do they do it?

You will learn how they do it in these pages. Using a series of case studies to illustrate key takeaways, we clearly identify and explain the essential core elements of project management and how to plan and control projects successfully. These valuable principles enable project managers and their teams to rapidly and successfully:

- Form the project team and appoint the project manager.
- Define the project scope, objectives, constraints, and other key attributes.
- Analyze the work content.
- Assign responsibilities to team members.
- Develop the project schedule.
- Develop the resource plan for staff and other key resources.
- Develop the project budget
- Monitor and control project quality, progress, and cost.

Providing the missing link between strategy formulation and implementation, The Project Success Method is a blueprint for you to define, plan, and control your strategic projects for superior performance and reap the competitive benefits of project success.

You may be wondering why the subtitle of this book includes the phrase, "... in as Little as 5 Days." The point is that a newly formed project team can be trained in the Project Success Method and coached through the processes of defining and planning a fairly large and complex project in only five days. How do I know this is possible? I know because my colleagues and I have worked with thousands of project teams to accomplish that very thing on a wide variety of highly strategic projects in a broad array of industries. To be sure, the five days involve intensive work, but the payoff is huge.

Acknowledgments

I wish to recognize and thank A. P. (Dennis) Young and Dr. Thomas B. Clark—co-founders of Project Success Incorporated (formerly YCA)—for their pioneering work in developing, perfecting, teaching, and applying The Project Success Method^{SM}. I also express gratitude to the many clients and consultants of Project Success, Incorporated, who by working diligently together on thousands of complex projects since 1983, have proven the effectiveness of the methodology.

1

The Easier Way

During a coffee break at a business conference a few years ago, I fell into conversation with the executive vice president of a Fortune 100 company.

After a moment or two he read the company name on my name tag.

"So you help companies achieve success with their projects. That's a tall order," he said. "Who've you worked with?"

I mentioned some of the technology companies, manufacturers, and producers of various types of services with whom we had been engaged. I explained how we increasingly found ourselves helping organizations execute complex projects with project teams whose members live and work in countries all over the world, speak different native languages, and have very different cultural backgrounds.

"Projects are always challenging," he said. "Right now we've got several in process: We're relocating one of our key facilities overseas, we're implementing an enterprise-wide logistics management system, and we're in the middle of a strategic new product development. They're all running far behind schedule and way over our cost estimates. Frankly, I'm not confident that I'll be happy with the results of any of them, no matter how long they take or how much they cost."

Why *Do* Projects Fail?

Why indeed! I'd say most executives, project managers, and members of thousands of project teams around the globe have asked themselves that question many times.

My 20-plus years' experience as an engineer, a project manager, and a project management trainer and consultant have shown me that there are a few basic reasons why projects so often fail.

Projects Are Fundamentally Different from Processes.

Companies serve customers, generate revenue, and manage resources through *processes*—for marketing and sales, manufacturing and service delivery, distribution, administration, etc.

Processes are systematic and repeatable. That's where much of their power comes from. Managers and operating personnel master their organizational processes, so that the processes become highly effective and routine.

On the other hand, companies build competitive advantage by creating strategic change through the execution of *projects*. Projects aren't like processes. Projects are not routine, and they usually involve far more uncertainty. You can't manage projects in the same way you manage the routine, ongoing processes of the organization. By their very nature, projects pose a wide range of special challenges.

People Fail to Recognize the Special Challenges Involved in Managing Projects.

I believe that projects are more challenging than processes. They have special types of problems, and managing them effectively requires a special set of skills.

First, unlike ongoing processes, projects are supposed to have a beginning, middle, *and an end.* Typically, they must be completed by a certain date, and often project deadlines are extremely tight.

Second, projects may (and often do) involve a high degree of uncertainty about the specific work activities required, work methods, available resources, the durations of activities and their costs.

Projects often involve complex sequencing relationships among the activities. In other words, some activities cannot begin until certain other activities have been finished. Analyzing these sequencing relationships, especially for a large and complex project, can be extremely challenging.

Large projects may actually be a nested pyramid of projects within projects. So a given project may actually be a sub-project or a sub-sub-project within a larger initiative.

Projects frequently involve highly variable workloads for people and other resources. However, those resources typically have constant capacity, at least in the short run. This often leads to unanticipated overloads for individual resources.

Project teams differ from operational teams, too. Project teams are temporary and often extremely diverse. Team members may have different educational and professional backgrounds, use different jargon, and approach problems in different ways. They may even have different personal or organizational objectives.

In addition, project team members may be dispersed across the globe, making collaboration and coordination difficult. They may also be separated by language and cultural barriers.

Unlike in other areas of the business where lines of authority are clearly defined, the project manager may lack formal authority in relation to team members. It isn't uncommon for some team members to outrank the project manager in the organizational hierarchy.

Finally, because projects are non-routine by definition, they tend to invite changing priorities, miscommunication, confusion, frustration, and possible conflict within the project team.

Good Project Management Often Conflicts with Basic Human Nature.

Some of the most important disciplines and behaviors required for effective project management are contrary to fundamental aspects of human nature.

We all tend to procrastinate to some degree. We tend to underestimate challenges that we perceive as being comfortably in the future. On the other hand, many of us overreact to problems immediately in front of us. As stated in a basic principle of time management, we confuse the "urgent" with the "important." We waste time on the former and put off dealing with the latter.

As you'll see later, when we discuss "Shifting the Worry Curve℠" rather than fighting human nature, The Project Success Method recognizes the realities of human nature and uses them to make project management easier and more effective.

People Tend to Overestimate Their Project Management Qualifications.

People who believe they are world-class project managers far outnumber those who really are. Many people think project management is "just common sense," and they fail to recognize the specialized skills and processes required to manage projects successfully.

Case Study: The Midas Touch Financial Group

The Midas Touch Financial Group, a mid-sized firm with offices in seven cities in the United States and Canada, is about to move its headquarters to leased space in a new building. Chief Operating Officer, Pat Crandall calls Office Manager, Chris Toliver into his office one morning.

"Chris, you know we're going to move the office soon," Crandall said as he seated himself behind his desk. "I've been thinking a lot about this move and how complex it is. With the corporate offices, the data center, and the customer service center moving, it's got the potential to be extremely disruptive to our operations."

"Every functional department in the organization will be involved and affected, and I want to make sure that we pull this off with the minimum possible disruption. To do that, I want to treat this move as a formal project, which means I need a strong project manager," Crandall said.

Toliver nodded. "You're right, Pat. I've been thinking about it, too. We need a solid plan and tight execution."

"Chris, I know you've only been with us for a few months, but I've been impressed with your planning and organizational skills. I know you've already got a full plate, but would you be willing and able to take on the job of managing this project? Obviously, it's a very high-profile job. It would give you a great opportunity to stand out, if you can manage the move successfully."

"Thank you, Pat. I appreciate your confidence in me," Toliver replied. "Yes, I'd like to take on the responsibility. I'm confident I can handle it."

"Great! Thanks for stepping up to the plate on this. By the way, have you had much experience managing projects?" asked Crandall.

* This case is fictitious. Any similiarity to actual, existing companies, individuals, or projects is purely coincidental.

(*continued*)

Again, Toliver nodded. "Yes, I've managed several projects during my career. Of course, they weren't as large as this one. They involved just me and one or two other people. But as I see it, project management is mainly common sense. It's not rocket science."

"I agree; it's not rocket science. But have you had any training in project management?" asked Crandall.

"Several years ago I took a one-day project management class offered by the local chapter of the American Association of Program and Project Managers," said Toliver. "It covered things like bar chart schedules and something called earned value analysis."

He paused. "I think I still have the notebook from that class somewhere in my files. I still haven't unpacked everything from my move from San Francisco. I'll see if I can put my hands on it tonight."

"I've also played around a little with the Project Pilot software we've got on our server. That may be useful. I think I saw a tutorial on it somewhere," Toliver added. "Don't worry, Pat. I can handle this project. The move will go like clockwork."

Crandall stood up. "Thanks Chris, I appreciate your willingness to take on the extra work, and I'm happy to see you're confident," he said, shaking Toliver's hand. "That's one less thing for me to worry about. And don't you worry. I'll be here to support you any way I can."

Questions

1. Based on this conversation, how confident are you about Chris Toliver's qualifications to manage this project? What led you to this conclusion?
2. What additional questions should Pat Crandall have asked to understand Toliver's qualifications?

I've seen it many times. Just as Chris does in the case study above, people frequently overestimate their own ability to manage projects for a wide variety of reasons.

- People don't know what they don't know. They don't realize that proven management processes exist for defining, planning, and controlling projects. If they aren't aware of these management processes, they can't be aware of their own deficiencies in project management know-how. Agreed, successful project management isn't rocket science. But you do need the specific knowledge of these project management processes as well as the skills and tools necessary to apply them effectively.
- Many of the short courses in project management among the plethora offered by colleges, training firms, and professional associations are a mile wide and an inch deep. These courses give participants a false sense of expertise.

In theory, there is no difference between theory and practice. In practice, there is.

—Yogi Berra

The courses typically introduce students to a broad array of project management techniques, but they don't explain how these techniques fit into the processes that are used to define, plan, and control projects. They don't explain the importance of each technique in those processes. They seldom provide practice in developing the analytical skills students need to apply the techniques correctly, nor do they warn students of the potential errors and pitfalls of each technique. Students are left with superficial knowledge of many techniques and little understanding of why, when, and how to use them. Too often the instructors who teach these short courses have little significant experience managing real business projects. Their material may be out of date or of little practical value. As a result, students still "don't know what they don't know," when they complete the course. Unfortunately, many of the instructors don't know either.

- People tend to equate superficial knowledge of project management software with in-depth knowledge of project management itself. Tiger Woods probably uses the best golf clubs money can buy, but his clubs don't make him a great golfer. Louis Armstrong's trumpet wasn't the reason he was a revolutionary figure in American jazz. Similarly, project management software is not the key to being a world-class project manager. Most courses and tutorials on project management software simply introduce students to the software's features and where to click the mouse to make the software do certain things. They barely mention—if at all—the project management processes the software was designed to support. Yet often people with a rudimentary knowledge of a project management software tool believe they know all about project management. In the hands of an untrained project manager, that software can be more dangerous than helpful to a project.
- Project managers tend to overvalue their past project management experience.

Practice does not make perfect. Only perfect practice makes perfect.

—Vince Lombardi

Experience is a great teacher—if you've been learning the right lessons. Just because an individual has managed projects for ten years doesn't mean that he or she has done so correctly or successfully. Has this project manager achieved the desired results? Were the projects relatively small and/or simple, so that the experience isn't a meaningful qualification for the larger and more complex project at hand? The only experience that is a valid qualification for project management competence is the successful application of proven project management processes on projects of significant size and complexity.

- Even earning a master's degree or a formal certification in project management is no guarantee that an individual is a competent project manager. However, such credentials lead people to believe they have real-world skills, when what they've got is book knowledge and theory. I know this will be heresy to some, but I have met too many people with such credentials who cannot manage projects successfully. Yes, anyone who has acquired the credential has demonstrated the personal commitment and the initiative necessary to jump through the required hoops. But does passing an exam demonstrate mastery of project management processes? Is there any assurance the candidate has successful experience applying the techniques he or she has been taught?

Make *Your* Project Succeed!

You can acquire the skills you need to effectively manage large, complex projects in the fast-paced, rapidly changing, highly competitive 24/7 global marketplace and arm your organization with the power of the Project Success Method.

We've worked in companies as diverse as Alltel, Caterpillar, The Coca-Cola Company, Delta Air Lines, Disney, Fujitsu, Ingersoll Rand, Kimberly-Clark, Marriott, Radio Shack, TRW, and Turner Broadcasting.

In all of the industries represented by these firms, and in virtually any other endeavor I can think of, the dominant organizations are those that consistently are more agile than their competition. They develop and launch new products, technologies, systems, and strategic programs more quickly and more efficiently than their competitors. They open new facilities faster. They forge winning mergers and acquisitions, develop marketing campaigns, and stage special events that leave the competition in the dust.

These are the companies that have developed the knowledge, skills, tools, and systems required to manage projects successfully. They are effective because they know what tools and techniques really work to manage projects. They understand the principles that generate the project power to overcome the inevitable, dynamic challenges that any large, complex project will involve.

They've learned the tested, proven principles that underlie The Project Success Method. This methodology was developed by A. P. (Dennis) Young and Dr. Thomas B. Clark, who were the co-founders of our firm. The effectiveness of The Project Success Method has been proven by its application to thousands of our clients' complex, business-critical projects since 1983.

What Is The Project Success Method?

The Project Success Method is quite simply a way to manage projects that has been honed to the essentials and sharply focused on achieving positive results in all three areas of project performance: *Quality*, *Time*, and *Cost*.

The Project Success Method will give you and your organization the key principles and management processes you need to manage projects effectively, achieve success, and empower team members to experience a sense of accomplishment and take pride in their work.

Having the ability to execute projects more effectively, faster, and at lower cost than your competition generates competitive advantage. Your organization will be more nimble, more responsive to customers and markets, and better able to compete in today's demanding, fast-moving global economy.

As an individual who has the skills to lead successful projects, you will enjoy a personal competitive advantage, too. Effective project leaders are more valued today than ever, especially when their success is clearly the result of applying a structured, disciplined approach like The Project Success Method.

Fail to manage projects effectively and the reverse will be true. Your company will be at a competitive disadvantage. You will be ineffective in meeting customers' needs. You will waste time and money. You, your associates, and employees will be dissatisfied and professionally unfulfilled.

Almost three decades ago, Tom Peters, co-author of *In Search of Excellence*, predicted that the ability to execute projects successfully would become an unparalleled source of competitive advantage. Events have proven how right he was. The power that flows from the ability to manage projects successfully is real. If you don't have it, you are at a significant disadvantage to those who do.

That power is here, in The Project Success Method.

You're probably asking yourself, how can this little book tell me what I need to know about project management, when there are bookshelves full of thick textbooks on the subject?

The Project Success Method will provide you with everything you need to manage projects, because in the practice of project management, as in pretty much every other area, the 80/20 Rule (or Pareto Principle) applies. Only here, it's more like the 90/10 Rule. Some 90 percent of the content you find in those thick project management textbooks is superfluous and of little value on most projects. The Project Success Method focuses on the 10 percent that is essential to success.

We call The Project Success Method "the easier way," because it is the most direct route to managing projects effectively. We formulated The Project Success Method to work in the real world, from real-world experience.

The Project Success Method is project management stripped of its unessential baggage. It is what you really need to know to manage your projects successfully. Learn it and be successful!

Key Takeaways

- Companies run day-to-day on well-defined *processes.* Companies use *projects* to create competitive advantage through strategic change.
- Projects fail for a few basic reasons.
- Be skeptical of the claims other individuals make about their project management expertise. Demand to see evidence that they have effectively applied proven project management processes to achieve success on projects of significant size and complexity.
- The key to managing projects successfully is to master a proven, structured, disciplined approach to defining, planning, and controlling complex projects—The Project Success Method.
- Individuals who have the skills to lead successful projects are highly valued in organizations, and they enjoy a competitive advantage over their peers.
- Some 90 percent of the real value of project management knowledge comes from a small number of key principles. These are embodied in The Project Success Method.

2

Master the Method

You're not alone in thinking that the challenges to managing projects successfully are formidable. Chances are, they are even greater and more numerous than you think.

In an informal survey, I have asked executives what percentage of the projects undertaken by their organizations in recent years were successful.

Their usual answer was from **70 to 90 percent**, which seems surprisingly high.

Upon further investigation, I have found that the answer depends on the individual's definition of "project success." When I defined project success as:

> Deliverables meet customer's requirements and expectations, *and*
> Project is completed on time, *and*
> Project is completed within budget . . .

the response from the same group of executives was only **5 to 20 percent**.

As a project manager and consultant, I've encountered many projects that were in trouble and in danger of failing completely. I've met a lot of credentialed project managers who desperately needed workable, real-world solutions to wrestle their floundering projects from the jaws of impending defeat.

I've also proven—with results in hundreds of projects—that there is an easier way to manage projects, one that vastly improves the likelihood of project success. There is a simple key to overcoming the challenges of effective project management.

You must master and commit to the disciplined application of management processes to forge four essential ingredients for project management success:

1. Build a real project team.
2. Concisely define project requirements.
3. Develop a comprehensive project plan.
4. Persistently control the project throughout its execution.

"Sure," you say, "mastering those processes is *what* I need to achieve project success, but that doesn't tell me anything about *how* to do it."

Luckily, the answer to that question is uncomplicated and easy to see in the life and career of virtually everyone who has achieved greatness in their endeavors, whether in sports, the arts, or business.

Let's take another look at Tiger Woods. Tiger is one of the greatest golfers who has ever lived. He makes playing the notoriously difficult and frustrating game of golf look easy. As any of us who've ever tried to hit a golf ball know, it most certainly is not easy.

But golf *is* easy for Tiger, because he's practiced many hours a day, almost every day since childhood. Tiger has great natural ability and enormous talent, but it was the consistent coaching by his father Earl, from the time Tiger was old enough to hold toy golf clubs, that helped Tiger make full use of his natural abilities and his potential to become one of the world's greatest golfers.

Talent paved the way, but Tiger achieved mastery of the game of golf through the same process you can use to achieve mastery in project management. What's needed?

- **Commitment** must come first.

  Unless commitment is made, there are only promises and hopes; but no plans.

  —Peter Drucker

  You may want to be a successful project manager. You may be interested in learning the techniques of effective project management, but unless you're committed to learning—and diligently applying—the principles of successful project management, you will never master the discipline.
- **Intensive training** on proven, practical project management processes and techniques is required.
  - The focus should be on the essential processes used to define, plan, and control projects.
  - The instructor must be a qualified project manager with credible experience applying the processes being taught.
  - Where training on project management software is needed, the training is organized around the project management processes that the software supports, not around the features of the tool.
  - This initial training should require no more than two to three days, because it is sharply focused only on the essential and most valuable project management knowledge.
- **Coaching**, again, by a qualified project manager, is vital.
  - The focus is on making the immediate transition from classroom learning to the application of that learning to real-world projects.

- The coach provides general guidance, enforces process discipline, and prevents common errors from creeping into the process.
- The coach remains available to provide guidance, once the project plan is fully developed, and the project is successfully executed through regular control cycles.

Follow these three steps, and you will become an effective project manager with The Project Success Method.

The Project Success Method: Three Management Processes

You'll remember I said that The Project Success Method was the easier way, because it was stripped down to what really works to achieve project success in the real world. The heart of The Project Success Method consists of three management processes that embody the essentials of project management.

1. FirstStep Process[SM]

   In the FirstStep process, we:

   a. Appoint a skilled project manager/leader.
   b. Form the project team with representation from every functional area involved in the project.
   c. Develop the project charter, which is a management (*not* technical) document that clearly and concisely defines the project requirements.

   By developing the project charter, the team and other stakeholders achieve consensus on the scope, objectives, constraints, assumptions and risks of the project.

   The FirstStep process builds the foundation for the planning process.

2. Planning Process

   The team develops its *plan* for *its project* to ensure that:

   a. The plan is really workable.

   b. The team is committed to the plan.

   The planning process is comprehensive and tightly integrated. It addresses the quality, time, and cost dimensions of the project in that logical sequence.

   The planning process involves:

   a. Breaking the project down into manageable activities (or tasks) and assigning responsibility for each activity to a member of the project team.

   b. Developing the project schedule using an approach that is far superior to the approach most people use, which is back-scheduling from the deadline. Our approach is explained in detail later in this book. We call it "forward scheduling and selective compression." The beauty of our approach is that you end up with a schedule that meets or beats the project deadline, avoids wasting money or creating unnecessary stress and, most important, results in team commitment to the schedule.

   c. Ensuring that resources will be available as required to execute the schedule.

   d. Developing the project budget and cash flow plan, if required. To be candid, this aspect of the planning process is more important in some project situations than in others.

   The team's commitment to the plan is key to the successful execution of the plan.

3. Control Process

   Control involves:

   a. Monitoring project performance for unfavorable deviations from the plan.

   b. Taking immediate corrective action as necessary to eliminate the unfavorable deviations.

Proactive identification and resolution of problems is essential to controlling the project.

Problem solving and decision making must be fact-based and involve the team.

Keeping the plan up to date and reinforcing the team's commitment to the plan are essential to success.

The Project Success Method is engineered to maximize the ten factors that my experience has shown most increase the likelihood of project success.

1. Active involvement by project stakeholders.
2. Capable project manager and team members.
3. A truly cross-functional team.
4. A team-based approach to defining, planning, and controlling the project.
5. Clear requirements and expectations.
6. Ownership and commitment by all stakeholders.
7. Early planning and early start of project execution.
8. Schedule based on a network diagram that captures the sequencing requirements among the activities.
9. Forward scheduling and selective compression (versus back-scheduling from the deadline).
10. Disciplined control process.

The Project Success Method has been honed by direct experience on thousands of strategic projects. The principles, processes, techniques and tools of The Project Success Method provide everything you and your organization need to achieve success in all three project dimensions: quality, time, and cost.

The Project Success Method *is* the easier way to manage projects effectively. It can be learned and implemented quickly. It's efficient. It has worked for thousands of project managers we've trained and coached. It will work for you.

Fast, efficient, practical, and proven. That's why we call The Project Success Method the easier way.

Key Takeaways

- The key to managing projects successfully is to master a proven, structured, disciplined approach to defining, planning, and controlling complex projects.
- In the long run, the easier way to perform any challenging feat is to master the skills needed to do it effectively.
- Develop your own project management capability as well as the capability of your personnel by mastering (through training and coached application) proven processes for defining, planning, and controlling projects.
- Apply those proven management processes rigorously and consistently, and expect your personnel to do the same.

3

Shift the Worry Curve

Just like project customers in general, your project customers (whether they be internal or external to your organization) expect total project success. That means they will evaluate the results of your projects on three basic dimensions of performance: *Quality*, *Time*, and *Cost*.

Your project customers aren't willing to accept success on one or two of these performance dimensions. They want it all! To satisfy them, you will have to complete projects:

- In accordance with specifications,
- On schedule, and
- Within budget.

That's what I mean by "project success."

And to consistently satisfy your project customers, you must commit yourself to the twin goals of:

- Instilling the drive for total project success in every member of your project team, and
- Applying management processes that maximize the likelihood of achieving total project success.

The Project Success Method empowers you to achieve both of these goals.

As the result of years of experience managing large and complex projects, I came to recognize a fact that I later incorporated as a fundamental principle of The Project Success Method: **Effective management of just one of the three dimensions of project performance is vital to achieving success in all three.**

In other words, if you manage one of the dimensions effectively, you greatly increase your chances of success on the other two. The reverse is also true. If you fail to manage the vital dimension, you will have virtually no chance of success on the other two.

Which of the three dimensions is the key and why? Let's imagine this all-too-common scenario.

The Typical Project

A company must execute a strategically important project, such as the development and introduction of a new product or marketing program.

The project is similar to projects that have been performed in the past, so project stakeholders believe that the scope, objectives, and constraints are clear, although they have not been discussed in depth or clearly documented. A deadline has been set twelve months hence, and that seems like plenty of time to get the job done. A team has been assigned to work on the project, and each team member thinks he or she knows what is expected, based on the functional area each represents. For all these reasons, no formal project planning or control processes seem necessary.

The level of concern, anxiety, or worry the project team members experience about this project will fluctuate over time in a predictable pattern, as shown in Figure 3.1. This pattern is an example of those tendencies of basic human nature we talked about in Chapter 1, a tendency to procrastinate and a tendency to underestimate future challenges.

The sooner I fall behind, the more time I have to catch up.

—Anonymous

At the start of the project, the typical team member will have a very low worry level for two reasons. First, there really is plenty of time to get the project done, and there is always more pressing work to get done in the immediate future. Second, because of the lack of planning, the team as a whole hasn't been required to think carefully about the challenge it faces. In all likelihood, team members have seriously underestimated the project's scope and complexity.

This honeymoon period, which I call the period of "uninformed optimism," may continue halfway to the project

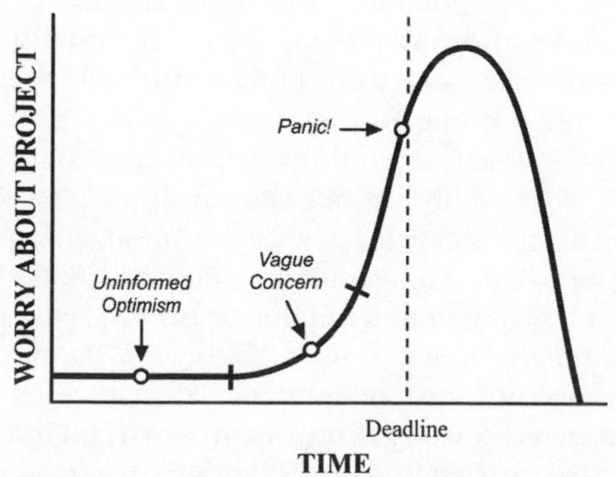

FIGURE 3.1 The "Worry Curve" Before Shifting

deadline or even longer. During this period, work may be delayed as uncertainties arise about specific project requirements, and project stakeholders are slow to clarify expectations. Problems arise, but they are not immediately recognized or addressed. Team members don't know how much trouble they're in, because there is no management system to focus their attention on the status of the project and the problems they need to solve. Everyone—the project customer, the project manager and each team member—is more than happy to postpone worry about this project.

As the project deadline begins to creep over the horizon, the project team gradually enters the period of "vague concern." Team members get a queasy feeling in the pit of their stomachs every time they think about the project, so being human, they try not to think about it. Team cohesion cracks as individuals start to take defensive actions—often finger pointing, which sparks conflict among team members in an effort to protect themselves from what they begin to perceive as impending doom.

Quickly, vague concern turns to "panic" as the project enters the third and final stage. The deadline arrives. The project is hopelessly behind schedule. The worry level shoots through the roof, and money starts flying out the door. The attitude becomes, "I don't care what it costs, just get it done." Under extreme pressure to complete the project, quality is compromised, as the team drops content and skips quality assurance steps. The stress on everyone becomes intolerable. The project ends in disaster. Competent, dedicated project team members lose their professional reputations, if not their jobs.

After surviving a project like this, most people vow never to let it happen again. "Next time, we'll use good, common sense," they say. "We will develop a plan for the project. We'll monitor the project and take corrective action as necessary—early, before problems get out of hand."

Unfortunately, most people find this is easier said than done. Ineffective project management is a vicious cycle that's extremely hard to break. While you're in a panic over one project, other projects are beginning, and under increasing pressure from the first project, you don't have the time to plan or control these new projects. The cycle repeats itself as each new project commences, and the organization is destined to go from one, out-of-control, panic-stricken project to the next.

This pattern of behavior is highly destructive. It damages the performance of the organization overall, and it creates an absolutely miserable work environment for individuals. It can, and often does, damage the careers and the physical and/or mental health of team members.

In my experience, it usually takes a senior manager to break this cycle. He or she must recognize the serious damage being done and finally say, "Enough! There *must* be a better way to run projects, and we're going to find it and use it."

Of course, there is a better way, The Project Success Method, which is also the easier way. Using The Project Success Method, the team works together to develop a project plan, and individual team members commit to specific, well-defined responsibilities. The team also commits to meeting regularly (say, every two weeks) throughout the project to report the status of current activities, to determine the status of the project, to solve problems as they arise, and to update the project plan. The results of this approach are shown in Figure 3.2.

Using The Project Success Method eliminates the period of "uninformed optimism," and the worry level starts at a higher level than in Figure 3.1 for two reasons.

1. The planning process itself raises the worry level, as the team analyzes the requirements, constraints, assumptions, and risks associated with the project. As a result, team members understand the challenges they face.
2. Team members also feel more pressure for progress from the very beginning of the project, because they know the team will meet, and they will have to report on their progress in just two weeks—and every two weeks after that.

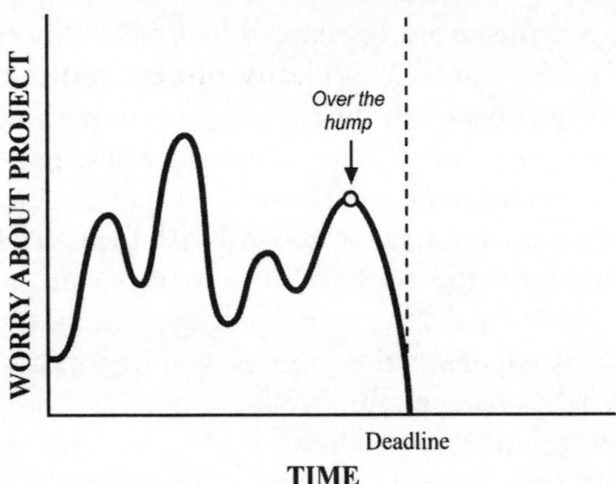

FIGURE 3.2 The "Worry Curve" After Shifting

Often, the project team will run into its first problem soon after the project begins. For example, the customer may change the project requirements, the team may lose a key member, or an unexpected technical issue may surface. Immediately, the worry level rises as the entire team swarms the problem. When they figure out how to overcome the problem, the worry level drops, at least until the team encounters the next problem.

Team members travel along the peaks and valleys of worry throughout the project as they encounter and solve each problem, instead of having to assault a Mount Everest of panic stage at the end of the project.

At some point, the team crosses "over the hump." The scariest parts of the project that involved the greatest risk and uncertainty are finished. Team members breathe a sigh of relief. There is still work to be done, but the team has the time, resources, and expertise needed to complete the project successfully. At this point, the project may even become fun, and the team may have the opportunity to enhance the quality of its project output beyond the customer's expectations.

In leading numerous projects, I've seen time after time that "worry" must begin early in a project, when it can and will be productive, rather than later, when the project team faces insurmountable obstacles. By using The Project Success Method to shift the worry curve, you clarify project requirements, you begin to realize progress immediately, you maintain team commitment and cohesiveness, you avoid panic, and you satisfy or exceed your customer's expectations.

Now compare Figures 3.1 and 3.2 with the three dimensions of project performance in mind. On the dimension of time, the comparison is obvious. The project in Figure 3.2 is completed by the deadline, whereas the project in Figure 3.1 ran over significantly. But what about the dimensions that aren't explicitly shown in the figures—quality and cost?

I know from experience, and I think you'll agree, that projects represented in Figure 3.2 will virtually always produce higher quality at lower cost than projects that run as in Figure 3.1. When projects are allowed to slide into panic mode, budgets are blown, and quality inevitably suffers in a desperate effort to finish the project.

Now, you decide. Which of the three basic dimensions of project performance is the key dimension? For me, there's no question: **The key dimension of project performance is TIME.**

"Hold on," you say, "How could anything be more important than quality?" It's not a matter of time being more important than quality. The dimension of project performance that is most important to the customer can vary from one project to another. More important, we define project success as meeting the customer's quality expectations, on time *and* within budget.

What I am saying is that if you do a good job managing the time dimension of your projects, you will maximize the probability of achieving success on the dimensions of quality and cost. Fail to manage the time dimension and your project will end up in panic mode, with quality sacrificed and costs exploding as you desperately scramble to finish the project.

The way to shift the worry curve is to focus on the time dimension of your project:

- Develop a workable schedule,
- Control progress against the schedule, and
- Update the schedule as necessary.

It works every time, and it's the easier way.

Key Takeaways

- The three dimensions of project performance are quality, time, and cost.
- Project customers expect complete project success—projects that are completed in accordance with specifications, on time, and within budget.
- Disciplined project planning and control processes shift the worry curve, so that panic is avoided at the end of the project.
- Effective management of the time dimension is the *key* to success on all three dimensions of project performance.

4

Build a *Real* Project Team

Chapters 4 and 5 address the FirstStep Process^{SM}. In this chapter, we will look at issues related to forming the project team and appointing the project manager. In Chapter 5, I will describe and illustrate the development of the project charter to define the requirements and other key attributes of the project.

Today, organizations of every kind and size recognize the critical importance of effective teams to their success. Scores of books from management gurus such as Kenneth Blanchard (*The One Minute Manager Builds High-Performing Teams*), Jon Katzenbach (*The Wisdom of Teams*), and many others crowd the market. Yet the success of so many of these books offers solid evidence that team building continues to be a tough challenge for many organizations. On the next page, consider the situation at the fictional company, The Midas Touch Financial Group (first introduced in Chapter 1).

Which do you think comes first—the creation of a team or the performance of teamwork? The answer seems obvious to

Case Study: The Midas Touch Financial Group

The Midas Touch Financial Group has formed a project team to handle moving its headquarters to a leased space in a new building. The team is in the initial stage of the project, when team member Brooke Davis (Assistant Manager, Customer Service Department) has lunch one day with a friend, Julio Rivera.

"Brooke, I hear you're on the project team for the office move to the new building," said Julio, as they waited for their food.

"Yeah, I guess so; that is, if you can really call it a 'team,' " she replied.

"Oh, that doesn't sound good. What do you mean by that?"

"Well, we had our first team meeting this morning," Brooke said. "There are people on the team from every department, and I don't know a lot of them. They appointed Chris Toliver the project manager. Do you know him? He's only been with the company for a few months. He had that 'deer in the headlights' look for most of the meeting," she said.

"So, what happened at the meeting?"

"Not much. They talked about how important it is for the move to go smoothly and not disrupt our operations. They emphasized that we have to move when we are supposed to. The schedule can't slip. But other than that, not much happened," Brooke said. She paused, and then continued.

"You know, I'm not sure what they expect from me, which is just fine with me. I have a ton of work and so much going on right now that I can't spend a lot of time on this project. I'd really like to stay out of it as much as possible."

* This case is fictitious. Any similiarity to actual, existing companies, individuals, or projects is purely coincidental.

Questions

1. Based on Brooke's comments, would you describe the project team for the headquarters move as a *real* team? What are the distinguishing characteristics of a real team?
2. What needs to happen for this project team to develop into a *real* team?

most people. First, you build the team, and then the team produces "teamwork." Right? Actually, it's the opposite. **Teamwork builds the team.**

This probably seems counterintuitive to you, but if you've ever been involved in forming a kids' baseball team to play in an organized league, or any similar endeavor, these dynamics of team building may be familiar to you.

Let's say the league rules allow up to 15 players per team. If you select 15 kids of the appropriate age, have you created a real baseball team? No? Suppose you give each child a baseball glove and a uniform with his or her name and number on the back and "Wild Cats" on the front. They look more like a team, but have you created a real team yet? Still no? Why not? What's missing?

Until this group of kids gets out on the field and starts to practice and play baseball together, it's not really a team. In other words, until they begin to engage in teamwork, they're not a real team.

This transition from a group of kids wearing uniforms to a real team doesn't happen automatically. You need a coach and a process of team development. Someone has to take the leadership role—to assign field positions to the individual team members, to develop a batting lineup, and to coach the team on the basics of the game. Then, and only then, do they have a chance at being a real team and performing real teamwork.

I believe the essence of any real team (in sports, in projects, in any endeavor) is *mutual accountability and support* in organized pursuit of a common goal.

Members of real teams realize that they will win or lose (succeed or fail) as a team, not as individuals. All team members understand what is expected of them. Nobody wants to let his or her teammates down by failing to perform, and team members are proactive in backing up their teammates.

As with our kids' baseball team, you can't build a project team simply by appointing individuals to the team. As I mentioned in Chapter 1, the project team is usually temporary and often consists of individuals from different functional areas or even different organizations. These people may have different educational backgrounds, use different professional jargon, approach problems in different ways, and likely have different personal or organizational objectives. Individuals may even want to minimize their involvement in the project, just as Brooke Davis does in the Midas Touch Financial Group case study.

To transform this diverse group of uncommitted people into a real team, you must have a process by which they are led to begin working together as a team. Fortunately, the processes of defining and planning the project, which take place in the earliest phase of The Project Success Method, are excellent vehicles for team building. When team members collaborate to develop the project definition and plan, the group begins to interact like a real team. Through this interaction—this teamwork—over time, individuals develop the mutual accountability and support in organized pursuit of a common goal that is the essence of a real team.

Coming together is a beginning. Keeping together is progress. Working together is success.

—Henry Ford

Again, this process does not happen automatically. Leadership is required, and the ideal source of that leadership is the project manager. The process should begin immediately after the team is formed, and it must be well structured, logical, efficient, and disciplined.

So, as counterintuitive as it may seem, developing teamwork actually does precede the creation of a real team. In fact, structured teamwork is essential to building a real team.

Now here's the good news. A cross-functional, team-based planning process serves two vital purposes at once. It is the best way to build a real project team, and it's also the best approach to building a good project plan. In fact, it is the only consistently effective approach to project planning I know of. Unfortunately, people tend to resist the process, as we can see in the case study below.

Case Study: Soaring Eagle Aircraft

Soaring Eagle Aircraft is about to start the development of a new model. The SEA82TJ will be a medium range, twin turboprop, eight-passenger plane, using state-of-the-art technology in all systems. John Moraitakis, a veteran Soaring Eagle senior engineer, has been named project manager. The team consists of representatives from every system area (airframe, avionics, hydraulics, propulsion, navigation, etc.) that will be involved in the project.

John Moraitakis watched the members of his newly formed project team arrive for their first planning session as a team. He waited until everyone got settled, then introduced himself.

* This case is fictitious. Any similarity to actual, existing companies, individuals, or projects is purely coincidental.

(*continued*)

"Thank you all for being here on time this morning. As you probably know, we have a lot of work to do, and it's important to get started right away. As those of you who've worked with me on previous projects know, I want us to work together as a team to develop our plan for this project," John explained. He paused when he saw team member Kristie Chung gesture to him. He nodded and pointed in her direction. "Yes, Kristie?"

"John, I appreciate your participative approach to project planning," Kristie said. "But given how busy we all are, I wonder if we can find an approach that won't take up so much of our time. I can't speak for the other members of the team, but I'd be happy to have you develop the project plan. You have lots of experience leading product development projects. I think you could develop a plan that would be just as good as one that we all worked on together. Besides, we can all review the plan when you're done, to see if there are any problems with it," she added.

"I agree with Kristie," Bob Whitaker quickly called from the back, eliciting a murmur of agreement throughout the room.

John held up his hand. "I appreciate your confidence in me, and I am very aware that we need to conserve your time. But I wouldn't consider trying to develop the plan myself. My technical expertise is pretty much limited to hydraulics and we need to make use of all the expertise in this room," he explained.

"Well, how about this approach?" Kristie asked. "What if each team member develops a plan for his or her system, then we can assemble the system-level plans into an overall project plan? At least we wouldn't have to sit through the planning for each other's systems."

Questions

1. How should John respond to Kristie's idea? Why?
2. What are the advantages of a cross-functional, team-based approach to project planning?
3. How can the cross-functional, team-based approach be made as efficient as possible?

Before discussing the virtues of a cross-functional, team-based approach to project planning, let's consider the problems associated with the two alternative approaches suggested by Kristie. People often view these alternative approaches as ways to conserve the team members' time in the planning process.

The first alternative is to have one person, usually the project manager, develop the plan and then allow the team to review it for any problems. This approach is neither team-based nor cross-functional.

An obvious problem with this approach is that the project manager may lack adequate expertise in some areas to develop a complete and workable plan. To the extent that team members discover errors and oversights that require the plan to be revised significantly, the planning process is likely to take longer to complete than if the entire team had been involved from the beginning.

Another potential problem is that the team members may not devote the time and attention necessary to review the plan carefully, so that planning errors and oversights aren't discovered until they show up during the actual execution of the project. We're dealing with human nature again. When people are motivated to minimize the time they devote to planning, they are often tempted to perform a cursory review and get on with the "real work" of the project.

The third problem is probably the most subtle and potentially the most devastating to ultimate project success. As explained earlier, the project definition and planning processes are excellent team-building opportunities. We want the team to develop the essence of a real team—mutual accountability and support in organized pursuit of a common goal. We want the individual team members to think of the project plan as *their plan* for *their project* (not the project manager's plan for the project manager's project). Removing the team from the planning process squanders this great opportunity to develop real team commitment.

The second alternative approach to planning is to have the representative(s) of each functional area on the team develop the plan for his or her own portion of the project and then assemble the functional plans into an overall project plan. This approach might be described as sub-team-based, but it's not truly cross-functional.

One danger here, of course, is "stovepipe" planning—the failure to recognize the interactions and interdependencies among the functional areas. For example, an activity in one functional area requires information that is an output of an activity in another functional area. If the plan fails to capture the precedence relationship between these activities, it will be unworkable.

Another potential problem with this approach is inconsistency throughout the plan in terms of quality, completeness, or structure. Some functional areas may never actually do the planning or may throw together a plan with minimum thought and effort just to get it done. Some functional groups may plan at a more detailed level than others. For example, one group may define activities with typical durations of a few days, while another uses activities with durations of several weeks. Some may use a network-based approach to scheduling their work, as explained later in this book (see Chapter 7), while others simply specify start and end dates for each activity. Different groups may use different project management software tools, and some may not use project management software at all. The problem of inconsistency among functional groups makes it extremely difficult, if not impossible, to assemble a coherent, overall cross-functional plan.

Finally, although this approach involves the team members in the planning process, it still fails to take advantage of the team-building aspects of a truly team-based, cross-functional approach, where all the team members work together to develop the plan.

There simply is no substitute for the team-based, cross-functional approach to project planning. This approach consistently leads to the development of the best plan and—even more important—the team's commitment to that plan. And it's the easier way!

However, this approach does involve an investment of the team members' time. To gain the team's support for the team-based, cross-functional approach, it's important for you to make the planning process as efficient as possible. Some keys to maximizing efficiency are:

- Use a planning process that is logical and involves minimal back-tracking. Each step in the process should "peel one layer of the onion" and provide an opportunity to catch errors and oversights before moving to the next step.
- Ensure that every member of the team is trained in the planning process. If not, you'll waste everybody's time, as you explain what you're doing in each step, as well as how and why you are doing it. In addition, people who do not understand the process tend to resist the process.
- To the extent that you repetitively perform similar projects, take advantage of the opportunity to develop and apply planning templates to avoid unnecessary effort. Always be careful when you use planning templates, however, to identify and adjust for the differences between the specific project at hand and the template, which is based on the typical project of that type.
- Within individual steps in the project planning process, it is often possible to delegate assignments to individuals or groups within the team, who can then work in parallel to speed up the process. For example, you can assign appropriate

sub-groups of team members the task of identifying the activities associated with specific project deliverables. Individual team members may estimate the durations, resource requirements, and costs of the specific activities that they are responsible for managing. However, be sure: (1) that such delegation only occurs within a process step, (2) that each sub-group is using a consistent approach, and (3) that the results of the delegated work are combined and reviewed by the entire team before moving on to the next step.

- Use the services of a project-planning analyst to facilitate/support the project manager and team in the planning effort. The planning analyst should be an expert in the project planning process and should be a power user of the project management software tool that is being employed. The analyst may be a staff person from the organization's project office (see Chapter 12 and Appendix G). Some project management consulting firms also provide this service.

Appoint a Capable Project Manager

The selection and appointment of a highly capable project manager is, of course, critical to the performance of your team and the success of your project.

In selecting the person to lead your project team, you should have clearly in mind the specific responsibilities that you expect the project manager to fulfill. Those responsibilities should include the following:

- Ensuring that the project scope, objectives, and other key attributes are clearly documented in the project charter
- Leading/facilitating the team through the project chartering and planning processes
- Acquiring (with the support of the project sponsor) the resources required to perform the project activities

- Providing technical guidance to the team as required
- Leading/facilitating the team through the project control process to:
  - Monitor project performance with respect to quality versus specifications, progress versus schedule, and cost versus budget
  - Identify problems and take corrective action as required
  - Update the plan
- Clearly communicating project status on a regular basis to all stakeholders
- Calmly and constructively managing disagreements, conflicts, and crises as required
- Performing other specific responsibilities (such as approving purchase requests) as required by organizational policy.

I recommend that you develop a job description for project managers that you can give to newly appointed project managers as well as their team members, so that everyone understands what is expected of the project manager. The job description should include each of the above responsibilities as a minimum. A good project manager:

In selecting a manager for a strategic project, look for a person with the characteristics, traits, and skills listed below. Before you read the list, let me forewarn you that individuals who possess all these characteristics, traits, and skills are extremely scarce. A good project manager:

- Is a member of the project team and will be significantly involved in the project with other team members on a day-to-day basis; does not stand above or apart from the team.
- Is recognized by the team members and other stakeholders as a person of unquestioned integrity; trusted to behave professionally and ethically.
- Is self-confident and willing to assume a leadership role; is action oriented.

- Understands the strategic business implications of the project, as well as the technical aspects.
- Understands and is committed to using the structured and disciplined processes of The Project Success Method to define, plan, and control the project.
- Possesses the leadership and facilitation skills required to guide a highly diverse, cross-functional team through the project definition, planning, and control processes; builds commitment.
- Is an outstanding communicator, both orally and in writing; is persuasive.
- Is personally well organized and disciplined; sets personal priorities and manages own time effectively.
- Is comfortable with and recognizes the benefits of an analytical, computer-assisted approach to project planning and control.
- Is creative in problem solving and encourages creativity in team members.
- Attends to detail and follows up as required.
- Is able to interface comfortably with both higher level managers and lower ranking operational personnel.
- Is flexible and adaptable; remains calm in a crisis.
- Possesses excellent interpersonal skills as required for coaching, motivating, team building, and conflict management.

Whenever you discover someone with all the above characteristics, traits, and skills, please let me know! I'm sure you can figure out why I would like to know about him or her.

As soon as the project manager has been selected and has accepted the assignment, senior management should formally announce the appointment to all interested parties. It is not fair to expect a project manager to step onto the project stage and assume his or her leadership role without proper introduction.

I also recommend that very soon after the appointment is announced, the newly appointed project manager, as his or her first official act in that role, immediately distribute a directory of team members showing appropriate contact information for each member. The directory should be updated and redistributed as changes may occur throughout the project.

Key Takeaways

- Never assume that you have a truly committed project team just because people have been assigned to work on your project.
- Insist on the team-based, cross-functional approach to project definition and planning. You will develop a superior plan, and this approach to project planning is effective in building team commitment to the plan.
- Remember that the team/commitment-building aspects of the project definition and planning processes are as important as the project definition and plan produced by those processes.
- Avoid the pitfalls of shortcut approaches to planning that reduce the involvement of team members in the process, no matter how fervently team members recommend those approaches to save time.
- Take appropriate actions to maximize the efficiency of the team-based, cross-functional approach to project planning.
- Ensure that the project manager's responsibilities are clearly understood by the project manager and other team members.
- Select a project manager who has the appropriate characteristics, traits, and skills.
- Once the project manager has been selected, senior management should make a formal announcement of the appointment, and the newly appointed project manager should take the reins immediately by distributing a directory of team members.

5

Charter for Clarity, Consensus, and Commitment

When a project team wades into the project without a documented and approved statement of the project requirements, the team takes its first steps toward failure. When after spending lots of time, effort, and money working on the project, it becomes painfully obvious that the project customer and the project team don't share the same understanding of the project definition, the downhill slide accelerates. The ensuing scramble to recover almost invariably leads to a failed project, interpersonal fault-finding, and damaged professional reputations.

Let's take a look at one of these typical disasters-in-the-making at New Millennium Manufacturing Company on the next page.

This case illustrates the very common and destructive phenomenon of "scope creep." Notice, however, that only the project manager and the team see the newly revealed requirements as an increase in project scope. The project customer does

Case Study: New Millennium Manufacturing Company

New Millennium Manufacturing Company is implementing the Galaxy enterprise management information system. Leslie McDonald (Chief Information Officer of New Millennium Manufacturing Company) finishes reading the latest status report on the Galaxy Implementation Project from Alex St. John (Project Manager), and then picks up the phone to call Alex. It rings just once before Alex answers.

"Good morning, Alex. This is Leslie. Listen, I just read your latest status report on the Galaxy Project, and I have a couple of concerns that I want to talk to you about."

"Oh? I thought you would be really pleased with the status of the project," Alex said, somewhat surprised. "We're right on schedule and running slightly under budget. It's been a pretty heroic effort, but everything seems to be going great, and the team's morale is sky-high. What are your concerns?"

"I was looking at the schedule for the remaining activities in the project, and I don't see any activities related to the user training component or the disaster recovery planning component of the project," Leslie said.

"That's because user training and disaster recovery planning were never considered to be within the scope of this project," Alex replied. "Our charge was to implement and integrate the software modules and the associated databases for the specific functional areas that you identified. You never mentioned user training or disaster recovery planning when you stated your expectations," he added.

"Maybe you don't consider those two components to be within the scope of the project, but I certainly do," Leslie

* This case is fictitious. Any similarity to actual, existing companies, individuals, or projects is purely coincidental.

said, tapping one finger on the desktop. "Your job is to implement the Galaxy system. User training and disaster recovery planning are certainly essential aspects of any system implementation, especially for a system as strategically important and complex as Galaxy."

"You're right, of course. I certainly agree that both user training and disaster recovery planning are essential," Alex said. "I just didn't think they were part of our team's responsibility. I guess I assumed that the Human Resources Department would handle the user training and that the Risk Management Department would do the disaster recovery planning."

"Well, Alex, rather than assuming, I wish you would have just asked," Leslie replied. "In any case, you need to get your project team together quickly to amend the project plan. By the way, I still expect you to hold to the same project deadline and budget constraint."

Questions

1. Which of the two characters should have prevented this situation from occurring?
2. What do you suppose will be the team's reaction when Alex explains the situation?
3. Do you expect this project to be completed successfully?
4. Could there be additional components of this project that still have not been revealed?

not perceive a change in scope, in that he or she typically thinks that the requirements should have been obvious from the beginning.

Most people believe that situations like this arise because communication fails between the project customer and the project team. The project customer thinks he or she has adequately communicated the project requirements to the team, and the team believes it knows what the customer expects. In fact, there's a significant difference between the customer's actual expectations and the team members' understanding of those expectations. Improved communication at the start of the project can prevent some of the problem from occurring, some of the time. But in reality, communication failures are responsible for only a small percentage of these situations.

There is no such thing as scope creep, only scope gallop.

—Anonymous

Far more typically, the project customer has failed to clearly and completely define the project requirements in his or her own mind. Perhaps the customer simply didn't take the time to think through the expectations for the project or assumed the team would figure it out. In many cases, the customer doesn't even possess the skills to specify the project requirements. For example, the customer may not know how, in general, to define "scope" for a project. My experience is that very few people have any idea how to define project scope adequately. This situation is especially common for projects in which the customer has no previous experience.

A more insidious—and quite common—cause of these situations is that the customer, consciously or subconsciously, is unwilling to commit to a clear and complete statement of project requirements. By keeping the expectations fuzzy, the customer thinks he or she is maintaining the prerogative to revise scope and other requirements as the project moves along. Of course, this strategy is self-defeating, since it sows the seeds of ultimate project failure.

Fortunately, there's a management technique that can prevent the disasters associated with unclear project requirements, and it is an integral part of the FirstStep Process within The Project Success Method:

The first task of a new project team is the development of a written charter that clearly defines project scope and other key project requirements.

Specific Purposes of Project Charters

The first and most obvious purpose of a project charter is that it ensures that all the project stakeholders formally agree on the project definition and have recorded that definition in writing. The charter protects the project team against uncontrolled scope creep and the other disasters awaiting project teams that begin their work with only a vague or assumed understanding of the project scope and other requirements.

As a project manager, you want to involve all project stakeholders directly in creating the project charter. Ideally, the customer will participate directly in developing the project charter. Whether the customer participates directly or not, you as a project manager are well advised to ask the customer and all other project stakeholders to sign the charter to show their personal acceptance and commitment to the project definition.

In other words, if the customer won't participate with the team in defining the project, then the team should define the project and put the responsibility on the customer to either accept their definition or revise it. If the customer decides later to expand project scope or modify other requirements, then the project team and the customer must go through a formal charter revision process, during which all project requirements and constraints are open to discussion, renegotiation, and possible modification.

Project managers and teams in the construction industry learned the importance of this lesson centuries ago. The signed agreement between the customer and the contractor clearly defines project scope based on plans and specifications. If the customer asks for an additional feature, the contractor and customer must negotiate the added fee for the increase in project scope as well as other revisions to the agreement, such as changes to the project's scheduled completion date. In effect, a "change order" on a construction project is a revision to the project charter.

In other types of projects, however, project teams too often fail to follow this prudent discipline. This failure is especially common when the project customer is within the same organization as the project team. Keep in mind that any conversation about project scope and other requirements—no matter how comprehensive and concise it may seem to you—is no substitute for a written document that is signed by the stakeholders.

Another advantage of involving the project customer in the chartering process is that it usually gets the project started earlier and gives the team the maximum amount of time to get the project done. I have seen many cases where everyone in an organization knows that there is a major project to be done, and maybe they have a year to get it done. But senior management consumes the first six months procrastinating and dithering on specifying the project scope and other requirements. The chartering process forces the customer to grapple with the issues associated with the project definition and to make the necessary decisions, so that the project team can get started with its work.

The project charter has two other important purposes, as well. First, the process of developing the charter is as important as the document itself. The charter development process is an excellent opportunity—coming as it does at the earliest stage of a project—to involve the new team in teamwork, which leads to the development of a real team as I described in Chapter 4. And because of their direct involvement in the chartering process, the team members begin to take ownership of the project; that is, they begin to think of the project as *our project*, rather than as someone else's project that I would like to have as little involvement in as possible. So the chartering process helps to build a real team and to build commitment to the project.

There's often a strong temptation to have one person draft the charter for review by all stakeholders. However, this "strawman" approach short-circuits the teamwork and commitment-building value of the chartering process. A far better approach is to have the stakeholders start with a nearly blank sheet of paper and develop the charter together. This approach virtually always leads to a better charter. All stakeholders are actively involved and their views are represented. The process highlights contentious issues and enables stakeholders to tackle and resolve them at the most advantageous time in the process; that is, at the very beginning.

Second, the project charter serves as an efficient and consistent means of communicating the project definition to people who were not involved in the charter development deliberations, such as people who join the project team later, contractors and other resources who will work on the project, or managers of the functional departments from which the team members are drawn.

Because the project charter is such an important communications device, you should ensure that it:

- Is concise. My basic rule is that the charter should never exceed three pages, plus attachments, and would ideally be two pages or less.
- Avoids using technical jargon and undefined acronyms that may not be understood by some readers.
- Is written as a *management* document rather than a technical specifications document.

Components of the Charter

To illustrate and explain the components of a project charter, I will discuss the example charter shown in Figure 5.1. The example is based on a case for developing a new manufacturing and warehousing facility in Melbourne, Australia, for the

Century Manufacturing Company

Melbourne Plant Development Project

Project Charter

16 May 2011 – Draft #4

Background

As stated in the CMC Corporate Strategy Committee report dated 5 April 2011, CMC will enter the southeastern Australia market against established competition. This facility development project will be executed simultaneously with a marketing project to prepare for the launch of a regional promotional/sales campaign.

Scope

A manufacturing and warehousing facility based on the standard CMC design will be established in the Melbourne metropolitan area.

Required project deliverables are:

- A leased building with adequate production, warehouse, and office space
- Full complement of production equipment with standard CMC safety and quality control modifications
- Materials for the first four weeks of production
- Trained personnel as required for the first 3 months of operation (one shift)
- An experienced plant manager

Required project phases are:

- Design facility
- Acquire facility resources
- Prepare and install facility resources

The project does *not* include the start-up of production operations. The project will be complete when the plant is ready to begin production operations under the direction of the plant manager.

Primary Objective

To provide production capacity to support estimated sales volume of AU$25,000,000 per year in the southeastern Australia market through 2012.

Secondary Objectives

- To provide initial excess production capacity to reduce the order backlog in the Jakarta Plant.
- To identify opportunities for cost-saving and time-reduction improvements to the CMC new facility development process.

Stakeholders

Project Customer:	Rebecca McGowan, Executive VP and Chair, CMC Corporate Strategy Committee

FIGURE 5.1 **Project Charter: Melbourne Plant Development Project**

Project Sponsor: Taylor Baxter, VP - International Operations
Project Manager: Pat Anders
Team Members: Lin Chang, International Legal
Consuelo Garcia, Procurement
Martina Karlsson, Industrial Engineering
Hiro Matsumoto, Production Operations
Rafael Moreno, Training
Ian Puckett, Human Resources
Victor Schmidt, Equipment Maintenance

Time Expectations

The project will begin on 23 May 2011 and must be completed no later than 26 August 2011— a period of seventy (70) working days. Because CMC is entering a market with established competition, timely completion is essential to maximize the strategic advantage of surprise.

Cost Expectations

Total project expenditures (capital purchases and expenses) are estimated as US $6,250,000.
The late penalty rate is estimated as $8,000 per workday.
The early savings rate is estimated as $6,000 per workday.

Constraints, Assumptions, and Risks

- All hourly operating personnel will be hired locally.
- A veteran CMC plant manager will be relocated to manage the Melbourne Plant.
- The facility design and staffing plan must conform to the current CMC New Facility Model.
- Only vendors and contractors listed on the current CMC Approved Vendor and Contractor Report will be used.
- CMC has no previous operating experience in the Melbourne area.

Stakeholder Signatures

Rebecca McGowan, Project Customer	Taylor Baxter, Project Sponsor
Pat Anders, Project Manager	Lin Chang
Consuela Garcia	Martina Karlsson
Hiro Matsumoto	Rafael Moreno
Ian Puckett	Victor Schmidt

FIGURE 5.1 (*Continued*)

Century Manufacturing Company. Although the company name, plant location, and other details of the case are fictitious, the case is based directly on a real project that was performed very successfully. I will use this case throughout the remainder of the book to illustrate the FirstStep planning and control processes.

First, notice the official **Project Name:** "Melbourne Plant Development Project." From the completion of the chartering process to the end of the project, the project should always be referred to by that name. I have seen cases where a project became known by two (or even more) names, and that led to endless confusion. I remember one case in particular in which a new enterprise-wide management information system was being developed. Some people in the organization referred to the project by the name that had been chosen for the new system. Others (mainly IT personnel and contractors) referred to the project by the name of the relational database platform on which the application was built. I was not the only person who was initially confused by the two names for the same project.

Another common mistake is the desire by some teams to use an acronym for the project name. The team will waste hours coming up with a project name that fits the "cool" acronym they are trying to use. Yet just a few short weeks later, most team members don't remember what the acronym is supposed to stand for. Even worse, some will invent new project titles that fit the acronym but are derogatory. Unless the team is trying to hide the intent of the project, I suggest simply giving the project a name that describes the end result of the project and avoiding the temptation to be slick.

Deciding on the project name is usually a non-threatening ice-breaker to get a chartering session started. The project name is usually descriptive as it is in the case example. Sometimes, however, a non-descriptive code name is used for either of two reasons. The first possible reason is security. The organization performing the project may not want the project name to indicate exactly what the project is. The other possible reason is that the team comes up with a clever code name (such as "Way Down Under Project"), and they use it just for the fun of it.

Notice also that the **Date and Draft Number** are shown. Of course, the charter is initially developed at the beginning of the project, but it may be formally revised several times at later dates. And every time the charter is developed or revised, you are likely to go through several drafts before you have a version that all stakeholders are willing to sign. I recommend that you save every draft from every development/revision session, so that you can refer back to them if necessary. To avoid any uncertainty or confusion about the source of any draft, you need to show on each draft the date on which it was developed and its position in the drafting sequence.

The **Background** section of the charter answers the question, "Where did this project come from?" You may want to predraft this section of the charter, but allow the stakeholders to review and revise it.

The **Scope** section is probably the most important component of the charter. This section must answer the questions: "*What* does the project team have to produce?" and "*What* does the project team have to *do*?" Based on my experience, I strongly recommend that these two dimensions of project scope be explicitly and separately addressed in the charter:

1. **Project deliverables or components.** These are the project outputs that the team is expected to produce. They are typically stated as nouns. So in the case example, the team is expected to deliver a *building*, *equipment*, *materials*, *operational personnel*, and a *plant manager*.
2. **Project phases.** These are the major stages of work through which the team is expected to carry the project. They are typically stated as verbs. So in the case example, the team must:
   a. *Design* the facility, which will include determining the requirements for specific equipment, floor space, and personnel and developing the facility/equipment layout.

b. *Acquire* the facility resources, which will include selecting and leasing the building; purchasing the equipment and the materials; recruiting, selecting, and hiring the operating personnel; and selecting the plant manager.

c. *Prepare and install* the facility resources, which will include installing an electrical system in the building, modifying and installing the equipment, training the operating personnel, and relocating the plant manager.

   One of the primary reasons for defining project phases is to nail down the definition of the end of the project. How will the project team know when they are finished? In a new product development project, for instance, exactly where does the development project end and the product management process begin?

Notice that the scope section begins with a one-sentence overview of the project scope. The section ends with a statement identifying any items that have been explicitly excluded from project scope, so that questions regarding those items do not come up repeatedly during the planning and execution of the project.

The **Objectives** sections explain the reasons or motivations for undertaking the project. The objectives are divided into *primary* versus *secondary* objectives. Typically, there is only one (or a very small number of) primary objective(s), which is the main strategic business reason for doing the project. The secondary objectives are things we hope to accomplish in addition to the primary objective, but we probably would not undertake the project just to accomplish the secondary objectives.

The objectives should be realistic, achievable, and measurable. The main reason for stating the objectives is to ensure that the project team fully understands why the project is strategically important.

A very common error in identifying the objectives (which should answer the question "Why?") is to simply restate the deliverable (which answers the question "What?"). For example, if the deliverable for a project is a new logistics management information system, the error would be stating the objective as "To develop a new logistics management information system." The objective should be something like "To increase inventory turns . . ." or "To reduce delivery delays . . ." or "To decrease transportation and inventory costs . . .".

In the **Stakeholders** section, we identify each of the following:

- The *project customer* is the individual for whom the project is being performed. From a customer satisfaction perspective, this is the person who must be satisfied with the outcome of the project. The customer may be external or internal to the organization that is performing the project. Sometimes it is tempting to identify an organization or group of people as the customer. For example, in a product development project, it would be tempting to identify the end users of the new product as the project customer. However, such an approach essentially leaves the actual, true customer out of the project management process, because the end users cannot speak for him or her. Instead, I strongly recommend that you identify an individual who will be responsible for representing or speaking for the organization or group. In the product development project, that individual would probably be someone from the marketing function, who should know what the end users want. Occasionally, a project may have more than one customer, but it should never be more than a small number.
- The *project sponsor* is a higher ranking (as compared to the project manager) executive in the organization that is performing the project. The sponsor has three primary responsibilities:
    - To ensure that the project manager is effectively managing the project. The project manager reports directly to the sponsor as far as his/her management responsibilities

on this project are concerned, even though the project manager may report to someone else in the organization on a day-to-day administrative basis.

  - To support the project manager and team in obtaining the resources and cooperation needed within the organization to execute the project.
  - To serve as the high-ranking representative of the project in dealing with the project customer.
  - In cases where the customer is internal to the organization performing the project, the customer may also be the sponsor.

- The *project manager* is the member of the project team who is responsible for leading the team through the processes of defining, planning, and controlling the project. The project manager is not expected to make all the decisions, solve all the problems, or do all the work, although he or she is typically deeply involved in all those efforts. In essence, the project manager is typically a player/coach for the team.
- The *team members* are the individuals who will participate directly in defining, planning, and controlling the project. They fall into two categories:
  - Most of them will be *activity managers*; that is, they will be responsible for managing the execution of one or more project activities. Note that this is a *management* responsibility. The question of who will actually perform the activity is a *resource* issue. The activity manager may also be the resource, but the activity may be performed by some other resource under the management of the team member.
  - Other members of the team will serve as *advisors*. They have special expertise, and their role is to provide professional guidance to the team, but not to manage activities. An attorney is a typical example on many project teams.

Incidentally, it is not unusual for the project customer and/or the project sponsor to also be members of the project team in either of the above roles.

The **Time Expectations** section states the expected completion date for the project as well as any major milestones (completion of phases) within the project. The expectations should be clearly stated as either target dates or absolute deadlines. In the case example, the completion date of 26 August 2011 is an absolute deadline.

The **Cost Expectations** section states the expected total cost of the project and may break the cost down into cost categories. Again, the expectations should be clearly stated as either targets or absolute constraints. In the case example, the total cost is expressed as an estimate, so it is a target.

Notice that the Cost Expectations section also specifies a *late penalty rate* and an *early savings rate*. We have all heard the expression, "Time is money," and that truism applies especially to projects. So if time is money, how much is a day worth on the project? The answer depends on where we are relative to the project deadline. The late penalty rate states the added cost for every day that the project extends beyond the deadline. I am not referring to the costs of performing the activities, since all the activities must be performed anyway, and the costs of performing them will be incurred regardless of when the project is completed. Rather, I am referring to project overhead and opportunity costs that are increased when a project runs late. Examples of project overhead are (1) the cost of managing the project and (2) the rent for general-purpose leased equipment, such as a tower crane on a construction project. Examples of opportunity costs are (1) the lost profit on a new product that is under development and (2) the lost savings that will be generated by a new information system that is under development. The early savings rate states the cost savings for every day that the project is finished ahead of the deadline. The same types of savings are involved, but the early savings rate is almost always a lower amount per day than the late penalty rate.

The main reason that we estimate and record these cost rates in the charter is to ensure that the members of the project team have a clear understanding of the value of time and how much they should be willing to spend to speed up the project. The team members are typically surprised by how large the cost rates are, mainly because they are often unaware of the magnitude of the opportunity costs. The values in the case example ($8,000 and $6,000) are relatively small compared to the cost rates we see on many strategic projects.

The **Constraints, Assumptions, and Risks** section is fairly self-explanatory. To the extent that the project team identifies worrisome issues at the beginning of the project, the more they will be able to develop plans that will minimize the potential negative impact of these issues. The most damaging problems on a project are typically the ones that are completely unexpected.

And finally, the project charter is not complete until every stakeholder identified in the charter has signed it.

The Charter Development Process

The most effective way by far to develop a project charter is in a meeting of the stakeholders. You need to do several things to prepare for the meeting.

First, give careful thought to who should be invited to participate. When in doubt about whether to include an individual, always err on the side of inclusion. I would far rather have a participant complain to me after the meeting that I should not have asked them to participate because they had no involvement (in which case I would apologize and thank them for coming) than to have a non-invitee point out a serious flaw in the project definition months after the project has started. Having said that, you and I both know that there are often people who you would much prefer not to invite. These are often people who know it all and love to hear themselves talk. They dominate every discussion. Or they may be naysayers, who are opposed to any new idea. These are usually the first people you need to put on your invitation list. Occasionally, they have something valuable to contribute to the discussion. Even if they don't, they will at least have had their say, and they will have seen consensus emerge around a different point of view. Otherwise, such people will be biting your ankles throughout the project.

You must carefully select a facilitator to lead the chartering meeting. The facilitator must have three characteristics:

1. The facilitator must thoroughly understand the contents and the value of a project charter.
2. The facilitator must have the facilitation skills necessary to lead a diverse group through a complex discussion that can become quite contentious. Make no mistake; leading a project chartering session is a very challenging, sometimes scary assignment. Many people simply do not possess the required facilitation skills or the courage. The facilitator must know how to encourage every participant to contribute and to think creatively. He or she must have the ability to gently but firmly control individuals who tend to dominate the discussion. And the facilitator must know how to guide the group toward achieving consensus.
3. Finally, the facilitator must be viewed by the participants as just a facilitator—*not* the person who is ultimately going to announce and impose the answer. For that reason, I would never ask the project customer, sponsor, or project manager to lead the meeting, although I definitely want them to participate in the discussion. When the sponsor, customer, or the project manager leads the meeting, especially if that person is a senior manager within the organization, the amount and creativity of the discussion is significantly reduced. Participants tend to sit quietly and wait for the facilitator to announce the answer. Why risk saying anything that might not align with the predetermined project definition? The participants tend to

regard the discussion as a charade that is intended to make them believe they are participating when in fact their input is not really wanted. If the project manager is forced to serve as facilitator, it is imperative that she or he has the other two characteristics described above. Otherwise, you should not set up the newly appointed project manager to fail in the facilitator role. I suggest that you find another good facilitator, even if that person has no other involvement in the project.

Estimate how much meeting time will be required to develop the charter. It always takes longer than I expect. In fact, my basic guideline is to come up with what I think is a generous estimate and then double it. Project chartering sessions seldom take less than two hours and sometimes require a full day of intensive discussion.

If charters for similar previous projects exist or if a template charter has been developed for this type of project, be sure to get those charters and review them carefully before the meeting.

An ideal approach to conducting the chartering meeting is for the facilitator to draft the charter on a computer in real time as the discussion proceeds. The document is projected on a screen, so that all participants can see it. When the meeting begins, the document may contain only the basic outline of section headings, a draft of the background section, and the signature lines at the end. The facilitator focuses the group's attention on one section of the charter at a time, but information that pertains to some other section may come up in the discussion at any time. The facilitator can easily scroll to the appropriate section of the charter to capture that information in the draft and then scroll back to the section under discussion.

Or the initial draft may be a fairly complete template, so that the discussion can focus on necessary modifications to the template, rather than reinventing the charter from scratch. It is important to note here, that this template would have been developed from previously completed projects of a similar, repetitive nature, and not, as discussed earlier in this section, a "straw-man" developed by one individual. A word of caution when using templates—ensure that the template is used only on similar projects and avoid the natural tendency to shoehorn every project that comes along into the template.

Occasionally, the facilitator may print and distribute copies of the current draft, so that the participants can see the complete document and write notes on it. I have found that distributing printed copies gives the participants a sense of progress toward consensus. It motivates them to finish the job and to get it right.

The objective of a chartering meeting is to develop a charter that every participant in the meeting is willing to sign, indicating his or her commitment to the project definition. However, there may be other stakeholders who did not participate in the charter development meeting. Those participants must review the charter and either sign it or request revisions. Sometimes it is necessary to have a follow-up meeting(s) to achieve consensus and commitment among all the stakeholders.

You may develop two or more different but consistent versions of the charter for a project for either of two reasons:

1. If you are performing the project for an external customer, the initial charter should address the project objectives from the customer's perspective; that is, why is the customer motivated to undertake this project. Once the charter has been developed, you should get the team together without the project customer and discuss the objectives from the perspective of the project team—for example, to make a certain amount of profit on the project. So you would end up with two versions of the charter. The version of the charter that the customer receives shows only the customer's objectives. The other version shows both the customer's objectives and the project team's objectives and is for internal distribution only.

2. The original version of the charter may contain confidential information that the project customer and/or team does not want to share with third parties who might receive a copy of the charter, such as contractors, vendors, or consultants. So a nonconfidential version of the charter is developed that can be shared with third parties.

Consequences of Inadequate Charters

Some project managers don't see the value in taking the time and effort to develop an adequate charter for their project. They may skip the chartering step altogether, assuming that all the stakeholders know and agree on the project definition. Or they may take a "quick and dirty" approach to get the charter done as quickly as possible. They may not involve the stakeholders in a meaningful way or seek their approval of the charter. Or they simply may not be capable of leading the development of an adequate charter.

Consider the probable consequences of launching a project without developing an adequate charter. They include, but are not necessarily limited to:

- No consensus among stakeholders on project scope, objectives, and constraints
- Lack of stakeholder commitment to the project
- Missed team-building opportunity
- No basis for project planning
- Unnecessarily delayed project start
- Uncontrolled scope creep
- Unanticipated risks/problems
- Wasted time, effort, and resources in project execution
- Loss of morale, stress, and conflict within the team
- Project failure with respect to quality, time, and cost
- Customer dissatisfaction

The probable consequences of the failure to develop an adequate charter are so dire that I sincerely offer the following advice:

If you use nothing else that you learn in this book (and I hope you will use the entire Project Success Method), *at least* develop an adequate charter for every project you undertake. That one management step will do more to prevent major problems and ensure project success than anything else you can do.

The project manager *must* take personal responsibility for ensuring that a clear and complete charter is developed and that the charter is formally approved by every stakeholder. If the project manager does not fulfill that responsibility, your project and your project team have been set up to fail.

Key Takeaways

- The failure to clearly define and document requirements at the beginning of a project is the single greatest cause of uncontrolled "scope creep" and other problems leading to project failure.
- Insist on the development of a project charter, even if the other project stakeholders feel that it is unnecessary. A verbal agreement on the project definition that has not been committed to writing is never sufficient.
- Involve the project team in the development of the project charter. You develop a better charter as a result of their involvement, and the chartering process is an excellent opportunity to begin building a real team, as well as building the team's commitment to the project.
- Use the chartering process to get the project started as early as possible, so that the team has the maximum amount of time to get the work done before the deadline.

- If the customer cannot or will not participate directly in the chartering process, have the team develop the charter and ask the customer to either approve it or revise it.
- Insist that all project stakeholders sign the charter, indicating their acceptance of and their commitment to the project definition.
- Use the charter as a concise way to communicate the project definition to people who were not involved in the charter-development process.
- The charter should address the project background, scope (deliverables and phases), objectives (primary and secondary), stakeholders, time expectations, cost expectations, constraints, assumptions, and risks.
- The charter development process involves an intense and well structured discussion among stakeholders led by a capable facilitator.
- The failure to develop an adequate project charter sets the project and the project team up to fail.

6

Break It Down and Divvy It Up

Once you've formed the project team, appointed the project manager, and defined the project through the development and approval of the project charter, the Project Success Method moves from the FirstStep process to the planning process. The first planning step is to break the project down into manageable activities and determine who will take responsibility for managing each one of them. The activities will become the building blocks of the project plan. On the next page, let's take a look at how Project Manager Alex St. John is handling this part of the Galaxy enterprise management information system implementation project at New Millennium Manufacturing (first introduced in Chapter 5).

Obviously, Alex has missed the mark. He's failed to achieve the two necessary requirements in this crucial first step of the project planning process:

1. Break the project down into manageable activities.
2. Identify which member of the project team will be responsible for managing the execution of each activity.

Case Study: New Millennium Manufacturing

Helen Groff, who is scheduled to teach a two-day user-training program on the Galaxy system starting tomorrow, knocks on Project Manager Alex St. John's office door one morning.

"Oh hi, Helen. Come on in," Alex said "Are you all set to start the class tomorrow morning? Some of our folks from Philadelphia and Seattle have already arrived, and they seem to be really pumped about the class."

Helen frowned. "*I'm* all set, Alex, but *we* have a big problem," she said.

"Really? What's the problem?"

"I was just down at the classroom checking things out, and I discovered that the room is reserved tomorrow for another class," she explained. "It's a user training class on a new computer-assisted engineering system."

"Didn't you reserve the classroom?" Alex asked.

"Didn't *I*? Now just a minute, Alex. You're not going to pin this foul-up on me. You asked me to develop the course and teach it," Helen replied. "I distinctly remember your saying you would have your secretary handle all of the logistical arrangements for the class," she added

"Sorry, Helen. That *is* what I said. Lynn reserved hotel rooms for the folks coming in from out of town, and she made arrangements for meals and refreshments. But I never thought to tell her to reserve the classroom. In fact, I see that we never even put the activity of reserving the classroom into the project plan," Alex said. "Could we move your class to another classroom or even take it off-site to a hotel meeting room?"

Helen shook her head. "No. We need access to work-stations that are connected directly to our network, and no

* This case is fictitious. Any similarity to actual, existing companies, individuals, or projects is purely coincidental.

other classroom is equipped with workstations. Of course, the engineering class also needs the workstations."

"Maybe the engineering folks could delay the start of their training for a couple of days and let us use the classroom, since we have participants from out of town. All the engineering people should be from here in Houston," Alex said.

"That's true, and I've already explored that possibility. Unfortunately, the instructor for the engineering class is a consultant from Boston, who arrived this afternoon. If they delay their class, he'll charge for his lost time, and we'll have to pay his fee and travel expense to bring him back again. Plus, he's not available to come back for at least six weeks," she explained.

Alex began to pace. "#&%*$+#! What are we going to do?"

Questions

1. Why do you suppose the task of reserving the classroom was never explicitly identified as an activity in the project?
2. If it had been identified as an activity, would the person responsible for the activity have been clear unless that person was specifically identified?
3. What costs—both tangible and intangible—will be incurred as a result of this foul-up?

The Work Breakdown Structure

We accomplish this crucial planning step by having the team develop a "*work breakdown structure*" (or "WBS") for the project. In developing the WBS, the team divides the project into smaller and smaller work packages until they ultimately get down to the

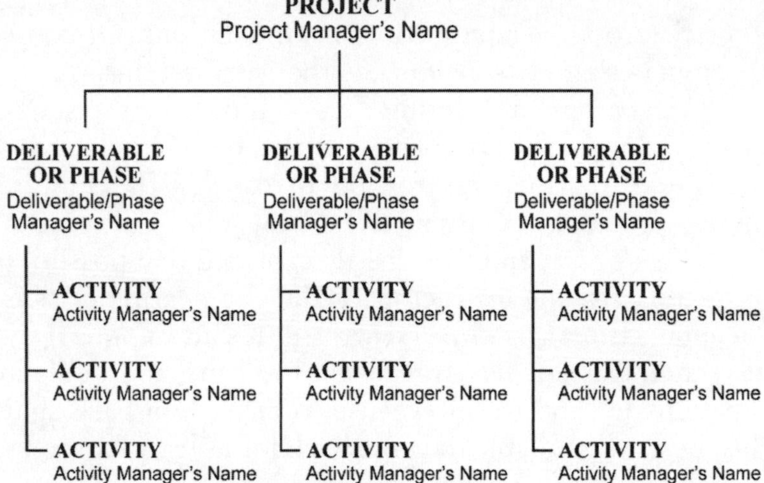

FIGURE 6.1 Work Breakdown Structure in Pyramid Format

manageable activities. Then the project manager asks individual team members to take responsibility for managing each of the work packages. Work breakdown structures are like snowflakes; no two teams would develop exactly the same WBS for the same project.

Figure 6.1 illustrates a small generic WBS in "pyramid format." The project name and project manager's name appear at the top of the WBS.

At the next level down, I strongly recommend that the project be broken down into *either* the *deliverables* or the *phases* that were identified in scope section of the charter. A common mistake at this level is to break the project down into functional areas (such as, engineering, marketing, production, human resources, information technology), which encourages a functional stovepipe approach to planning and executing the project. Remember that projects are inherently cross-functional, so breaking the project down into one of the two dimensions of scope maintains a cross-functional perspective. But how do you decide whether to break the project down into deliverables or phases? Usually, one of the two will be more distinct than the other. Referring back to the charter for the Melbourne Plant Development Project in Figure 5.1, I believe that the deliverables are more distinct than the phases. That tends to be the case in the majority of the projects. However, there are projects for which the phases (such as design, develop, test, . . .) are more distinct than the deliverables. Bottom line—let the team decide whether to break the project into deliverables or phases. Figure 6.1 also illustrates that a team member has been assigned to manage each of the deliverables or phases.

Sometimes in developing the WBS, the team identifies a project deliverable or phase that was not mentioned in the charter. In such cases, the project stakeholders need to decide whether that new deliverable or phase is within the intended scope of the project and, if so, formally revise and reapprove the charter.

At the bottom level of the WBS, the team breaks each deliverable or phase into the activities required to produce the deliverable or execute the phase. As I mentioned above, the activities will become the building blocks of the project plan (schedule, budget, etc.). The order in which the activities are listed is not significant. The WBS does *not* capture the sequencing relationships among the activities.

Before I say more about activities, let me show you another format for the WBS. Figure 6.2 illustrates the "outline format" for the same generic example shown in pyramid format in Figure 6.1. The outline format is generally easier to develop and more efficient to display, but the two formats contain exactly the same information.

Identifying the Activities

An **activity** (or "task") is any time-consuming element of the project that (1) has identifiable beginning and ending points and (2) contributes directly to the production of required project deliverables. In this case, "time-consuming" means that you

Work Breakdown Structure Outline Format	
PROJECT	Project Manager's Name
DELIVERABLE OR PHASE	Deliverable/Phase Manager's Name
ACTIVITY	Activity Manager's Name
ACTIVITY	Activity Manager's Name
ACTIVITY	Activity Manager's Name
DELIVERABLE OR PHASE	Deliverable/Phase Manager's Name
ACTIVITY	Activity Manager's Name
ACTIVITY	Activity Manager's Name
ACTIVITY	Activity Manager's Name
DELIVERABLE OR PHASE	Deliverable/Phase Manager's Name
ACTIVITY	Activity Manager's Name
ACTIVITY	Activity Manager's Name
ACTIVITY	Activity Manager's Name

FIGURE 6.2 Work Breakdown Structure in Outline Format

must provide time in the project schedule for the activity to be performed.

Two special cases are worth noting, because project teams often fail to recognize activities that have either or both of these characteristics:

1. Some activities consume time, but do not consume the productive resources (e.g., staff-hours) of the organization. For the project team, such activities involve waiting more than doing. Examples include:
   a. Waiting for a natural process to occur, such as the curing of concrete in a construction project or the cooling of a steam turbine in a power plant maintenance project.
   b. Waiting for some other organization to perform work, such as the production or delivery of items ordered from a vendor or an approval by the customer or a regulatory agency.

2. Some activities don't have an obvious end point. Examples include debugging a complex computer program and creative activities, such as designing a new company logo. You never really know for sure when you are finished.

Here's an example of an activity that has both of these special characteristics. Suppose you've mailed out questionnaires to 10,000 of your customers as part of a marketing research project. Now you have the activity: "Receive Questionnaire Responses." This activity is time-consuming in the project schedule, but it does not consume the productive resources of your organization. In addition, the end of the activity is unclear. If you plan to wait until all 10,000 questionnaires are returned, you'll be waiting forever. Therefore, you need to develop a definition of the end point, for example: "We will wait three weeks."

Again, the reason for stressing these special cases is that if you don't watch carefully for activities with these characteristics, there's a high probability they will fall through the cracks, and your project plan will be incomplete and unworkable.

How Much Detail?

One question that project teams always have when breaking the project down into its component activities is: How much detail is enough? Although there's no simple answer to this question, here are several guidelines:

- The level of detail should be consistent with the degree of control you require. In the project control process, you will track progress (and perhaps resource usage and cost) on every activity in your plan. So, in deciding whether to break an activity into greater detail, ask yourself whether you really need to track activities at the more detailed level. If you are not careful, you will end up spending too much of your time tracking too many activities at too low a level of detail.

- For each activity, one team member should be responsible for managing the activity and the same set of resources (i.e., people, equipment, etc.) should be used from the beginning to the end of the activity. If there's a point in the activity where a different team member should become responsible or different resources are required, then that activity should be broken into greater detail.
- Find a way to subdivide activities whose durations would otherwise be longer than about one month, so that you can track progress reliably. It's too easy to fall way behind schedule on long-duration activities and not realize the problem until it is too late to take corrective action. It's like shifting the worry curve at the activity level.
- Watch for activities whose durations are very short—perhaps just a few minutes—but that you need to include in the schedule as a reminder to perform the activity at the appropriate time. In general, such activities will have no impact on the schedule, *unless* you forget to perform them. However, if you do forget the activity, the results can be disastrous. Forgetting to reserve the classroom in the New Millennium Manufacturing case study is an example of such an activity. These activities often involve some form of communication.
- In long-duration projects, it is typically easier to identify activities near the beginning of the project in greater detail than it is to identify in detail activities that will occur farther in the future. In such cases, go ahead and identify the near-term activities in detail and the future activities in less detail (perhaps phases rather than activities). As you work through the project, you will be able to, and should, break the later activities into greater detail.
- Resist the temptation to micro-manage the work. Each activity should result in the production of a significant deliverable or a significant change in the status of the project. Allow the activity manager to figure out how to get it done.

He or she should be the expert anyway. The activity manager might even treat the activity as a subproject.

- I always hesitate to say this, but it may prove helpful to you in deciding on appropriate level of detail. I have found that there seems to be a "sweet spot" for the durations of activities in strategic projects. A large percentage of such activities fall in the range of 3 to 15 working days. Please, however, think of this range as general guidance only.

Both insufficient and excessive detail in identifying activities can lead to problems. My experience indicates that most people, when they first begin using formal project planning techniques, tend to err on the side of excessive detail. Experience is a good teacher here.

I've also found that a particular approach to naming activities helps to ensure their clarity and the appropriate level of detail. The approach I recommend is for the activity name to consist of an action word (verb) followed by the object of the action (noun). In other words, have the name answer the question, "What are you doing to what?" For example:

- Draft Script
- Test Code
- Install Equipment

It is also important that the activity description be just that—descriptive. Often team members will give the activity a very short name that makes complete sense at the time but no sense later. The reason is that when the team is developing the WBS, they are thinking in context; however, when the activity shows up on their "to-do" list weeks or months later this very short description provides insufficient information to complete the task. The team member will look at the activity with a puzzled expression and ask aloud, "Now, what does this activity mean?" I always recommend that the activity should be stated with enough verbosity that the affected team member would understand exactly what needed to be accomplished in order to mark the activity complete even if it showed up on his or her desk three months later in the form of a Post-It note. So to revisit the above examples:

- Draft Initial Script
- Test Code After Modifications
- Install Electrical Equipment in Warehouse A Control Room

A good way to check the completeness of your activity list is to ask, "Have we identified all the activities necessary to *produce all the deliverables* and *execute all the phases* specified in the project charter?"

Assigning Activity Managers

Now it is necessary for you to identify which member of the project team will take responsibility for managing the execution of the activity. Notice that the activity manager is not necessarily the person, or one of the people (i.e., the "resources"), who will actually perform the work. Instead, he or she is the person who is ultimately responsible for ensuring the activity is completed and reporting the activity progress back to the team on a regular basis. Each activity manager must be a member of the project team, meaning that he or she will participate directly in the planning and control processes for the project. Members of a well-developed project team will volunteer to manage appropriate activities or will readily agree to do so, when asked. When identifying activity managers, be careful to avoid these two common mistakes:

1. Identifying an external resource (such as a vendor or contractor) as the manager of an activity, when the vendor or

contractor is not actually a member of the team, but is simply the resource that will perform the work on the activity. You should have a member of the team who participates directly in the project planning and control processes and who is responsible for managing the external resource.

2. Identifying a person as the manager of an activity when that person has not yet been recruited onto the project team. Instead, recruit the person to join the team, and then ask him or her to take responsibility for managing the activity. Until an appropriate team member has been recruited, the project manager should be identified as the activity manager by default. This practice provides an ongoing reminder and motivator to the project manager to recruit the additional team members required. Most project teams grow as the WBS is developed and the need for additional team members becomes apparent. New team members should receive a copy of the charter and should be asked to sign the master copy to indicate that they are aware of the project definition and are committed to it. If the new team member sees a problem with the charter, the charter will probably need to be formally revised and reapproved.

WBS for the Melbourne Plant Development Project

Now that you know all about work breakdown structures in general, let's look at the WBS for the Melbourne Plant Development Project that was introduced in Chapter 5. Figure 6.3 on the next page shows the WBS in outline format.

Please notice how this example illustrates the following general characteristics of a well developed WBS:

- The WBS does not capture the sequencing relationships among the activities. For example, it is not obvious that

Century Manufacturing Company
Melbourne Plant Development Project
Work Breakdown Structure
17 May 2011

Task	Responsible
Melbourne Plant Development Project	Anders
Equipment	Victor Schmidt
Prepare Production Requirements Analysis	Martina Karlsson
Order Equipment	Consuelo Garcia
Assemble Equipment	Consuelo Garcia
Ocean Ship Equipment to Sydney	Consuelo Garcia
Install Equipment Safety/QC Modifications	Victor Schmidt
Rail Ship Equipment to Melbourne Plant	Victor Schmidt
Install/Certify Equipment	Martina Karlsson
Building	Martina Karlsson
Select Building	Taylor Baxter
Execute Building Lease	Lin Chang
Develop Plant/Equipment Layout	Martina Karlsson
Install Building Electrical System	Martina Karlsson
Materials	Consuelo Garcia
Order Start-up Materials	Consuelo Garcia
Truck Ship Materials to Melbourne Plant	Consuelo Garcia
Plant Manager & Operating Personnel	Ian Puckett
Select/Confirm Plant Manager	Taylor Baxter
Relocate Plant Manager	Plant Manager (TBD)
Run Help-Wanted Ads	Ian Puckett
Receive Job Applications	Ian Puckett
Interview/Select Personnel	Plant Manager (TBD)
Personnel Leadtime to Report	Ian Puckett
Train Personnel	Raphael Moreno

FIGURE 6.3 WBS for Melbourne Plant Development Project

the "Train Personnel" activity cannot begin until the "Install/Certify Equipment" activity, the "Truck Ship Materials to Melbourne Plant" activity, and the "Personnel Leadtime to Report" activity are all finished. The sequencing relationships among the activities will be analyzed and captured in a different type of diagram that I will explain in Chapter 7. The WBS serves only to identify the required activities and the activity managers.

- The project includes several special-case activities that involve waiting more than doing from the team's perspective. Examples include "Assemble Equipment" (which will be done by a vendor), the three shipping activities, and "Personnel Leadtime to Report."
- The project also contains at least one special-case activity ("Receive Job Applications") for which the end point is not obvious. The team will never be sure that all the applications have been received, but it can decide how long to let that activity run.
- The WBS provides a cross-functional view of the project and encourages a cross-functional approach to the work. Notice that in general, each deliverable involves activities managed by team members from several different functional areas of the organization. For example, the Equipment deliverable involves activities managed by Karlsson from Industrial Engineering, Garcia from Procurement, and Schmidt from Equipment Maintenance. Also in general, each team member is responsible for managing activities associated with more than one deliverable. For example, Karlsson will manage activities associated with both the Equipment and the Building.
- Finally, the position of a given person's name in the WBS is no indication of that person's relative rank in the organization. For example, Taylor Baxter (who is VP for International Operations and is the Project Sponsor) is shown as the activity manager for two activities. Baxter outranks

everybody else in the WBS, including the project manager, but that fact is not obvious from looking at the WBS. Showing relative organizational rank simply is not the purpose of the WBS.

Developing the Work Breakdown Structure

As with all other steps in the Project Success Method, the project team develops the WBS, because (1) the team will do the best job of identifying all the activities, (2) the process encourages the team members' ownership and commitment to *their plan* for *their project*, and (3) working together on the WBS is another opportunity to engage the group in teamwork that leads to the development of a *real team*.

Of course, we don't want to waste our team members' time, so we must take advantage of ways to make the WBS development process as efficient as possible, especially for large projects with lots of activities and lots of team members. As always, one way to speed up the process is to start with a template or with a WBS for a similar previous project. But be very careful to identify and adjust for any differences between the project at hand and the template or previous project. Another approach to gaining efficiency is to divide the team into groups and ask each group to identify the activities associated with a given deliverable or phase. You might also ask each team member to do some prep work and bring to the planning session a list of activities that he or she knows should be managed on each deliverable or phase. Eventually, the entire WBS must be assembled and examined by the team for possible omissions and/or duplications.

Allowing essential activities to fall through the cracks and/or failing to clearly establish which team member is responsible for managing each activity will disrupt a project, kill team morale, and lead to possible project failure. Having the team develop a work breakdown structure to ensure that all the required activities have been identified and that a team member has accepted the responsibility for managing each activity is *the easier way*.

For Advanced Discussion

A Related Problem and Solution for Projects Involving Several Organizations

One of the difficulties of managing projects that involve several (perhaps many) organizations is that the group has no pre-established procedures for handling actions that cross organizational boundaries. Such actions often include:

- Technical decisions (such as specification or design changes).
- Managerial decisions (such as schedule changes).
- Administrative processes (such as issuing payments for work).
- Project activities that involve more than one organization (such as approvals or inspections, placing purchase orders).

If such inter-organizational actions are not anticipated and procedures put in place to guide their performance, confusion and miscommunication will result, which will lead to unnecessary delays, wasted resources, and potential conflict among the organizations.

The development of operating procedures for multi-organizational projects can be facilitated by the use of a tool known as a "*linear responsibility chart*" (LRC). The application of the linear responsibility chart to develop operating procedures for projects involving several organizations is explained and illustrated in Appendix A.

Key Takeaways

- The purposes of developing a work breakdown structure are to break the project down into manageable activities and to identify the member of the project team who will be responsible for managing each activity.
- Maintain a cross-functional perspective in breaking the project down. Do not divide the project along functional lines. Instead, break it down first into either the deliverables or the phases identified in the scope section of the charter.
- The WBS can be displayed in the pyramid format or the outline format.
- Ensure that the project team has identified all the activities necessary to *produce all the deliverables* and *execute all the phases* specified in the project charter.
- Watch for activities that involve waiting rather than doing, and activities without obvious end points.
- Use the guidelines provided in this chapter to determine the appropriate level of detail in identifying the activities.
- Name activities using an action word (verb) followed by the object of the action (noun).
- As you identify a member of the project team who will be responsible for managing each activity, it may be necessary to add members to the team.
- Have the team develop the work breakdown structure for their project, but make the process as efficient as possible.

7

Network for Success

Even project managers with minimal experience recognize that a published schedule is a vital tool for managing any project. One common but highly flawed approach to creating and publishing a project schedule is to enter each activity name into a project management software tool along with the planned start date and duration for the activity. As the activities are entered, the software tool builds a project schedule in the form of a bar chart (or "Gantt" chart) with the activities displayed as bars on a time scale. Unfortunately, this flawed approach is widely used by experienced project managers, as well as by novices.

What are the problems with this straightforward and seemingly efficient approach? Let's see it in practice at OmniEnergy Enterprises on the following page.

Clearly, Charlene has a lot of work in front of her—and will have again and again—each time there is a change to the schedule.

In order to enter the start date and duration for each activity in the project, Charlene had to think through the sequencing requirements among the activities. However, she did not explicitly

Case Study: OmniEnergy Enterprises

OmniEnergy Enterprises (OEE) has signed an agreement to purchase Spirit Mountain Power Company, and the closing date for the transaction has been set. Charlene Jackson, OEE's Senior Attorney, is the project manager for the execution of the purchase. Charlene is meeting with Tony Castilla, OEE's Executive Vice President (and the project customer and sponsor) concerning the status of the project.

"Charlene, I really like the way you're managing this acquisition as a project. This bar chart schedule you created is clear and shows exactly where we're headed," Tony said.

"Thanks. I produced the bar chart schedule with the Project Pilot software. Actually, it's called a 'Gantt chart.' It's pretty easy to create. All you have to do is enter the start date and duration for each activity, and it creates the bar chart. It has lots of formatting options, too," Charlene added.

"So how are we doing so far?"

"To be candid, I am not quite sure," replied Charlene, shrugging her shoulders slightly. "I need to add a new activity to the schedule. As you know, our board has decided that we must perform special due diligence on Spirit Mountain's ownership interest in that nuclear power plant in France. It is an appropriate requirement, and we should have thought of it earlier. Plus, I have several activities that have finished later than planned."

Tony's eyes widened. "Uh-oh! Are those changes going to delay the closing date?"

"I don't know yet. I know they will delay some of the remaining activities, but not necessarily all of them. I'll just have to think through the project again, adjust the activity start dates, and figure out how the new activity and the late

* This case is fictitious. Any similarity to actual, existing companies, individuals, or projects is purely coincidental.

activities will impact the closing date," she said, shaking her head. "It's going to take some time to figure it out."

"Can't the Project Pilot software make those adjustments automatically?" Tony asked.

"I guess it should, but honestly, I don't know how to do that. I'm beginning to think that I am not using the full power of the software tool. As nice as this Gantt chart schedule looks, keeping the schedule up to date as things change is going to be a real hassle."

Questions

1. If Charlene is using a reasonably good project management software tool, why can't it automatically determine the impact of adding a new activity and/or late-finishing activities on the project schedule and completion date?
2. Considering the technique Charlene is using, do you think she will keep the project schedule up to date over the course of a fairly large, dynamic project?
3. What are the likely consequences if Charlene does not keep the schedule up to date?

capture the sequencing requirements in her project database. So, whenever there is a change to the schedule (such as the addition or deletion of an activity or an activity finishing earlier or later than its scheduled finish date), she must re-analyze the sequencing relationships among the activities and manually adjust the schedule to determine the overall impact of the change.

Such changes occur so frequently, and this approach to the schedule revision process is so laborious and cumbersome, that project managers often don't make the necessary revisions. As a result, the schedule soon loses its credibility and usefulness. The Gantt chart becomes nothing more than a wall decoration. It looks good, but nobody is paying any attention to it. From that point forward, the project manager and team cannot manage the time dimension of the project. And remember, the management of the time dimension is the key to overall success. If you want to decorate your walls, I suggest you get some travel or movie posters. They cost a lot less than the time it will take to develop a project schedule that cannot be easily updated.

Another less obvious problem with this approach is that it doesn't provide for the automatic identification of the critical path of the project, an extremely important concept that is explained in Chapter 9.

Develop a Project Network Diagram

A far more effective (and *easier*) approach is to explicitly capture the sequencing relationships among the activities in the form of a **project network diagram**, also known as a node diagram. Once you develop and enter the network diagram into the project management software tool, the tool can automatically update the schedule when changes occur.

The activities that we identified in the work breakdown structure are the building blocks of the network diagram. We use little boxes (called "nodes") to represent the activities. The boxes are all the same size; in other words, they are not scaled to the durations of the activities. As we analyze the sequencing (or "precedence") relationships among the activities, we add arrows between the boxes to depict those relationships. Figure 7.1 shows one type of precedence relationship. The "S" and "F" above each activity node mean that we think of the left side of each node as the start of the activity and the right side as the finish of the

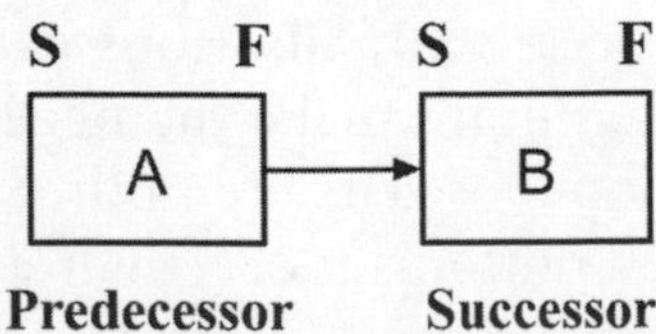

FIGURE 7.1 A Finish-to-Start (FS) Precedence Relationship

activity. This concept is understood, so that we don't need to show the S's and F's on a real project network diagram. The precedence relationship means exactly what it appears to mean, which is that activity B cannot start until activity A is finished. There is no duration associated with the precedence relationship, so B can start immediately after A is finished. Activity A would be referred to as the "predecessor" in this relationship, and activity B would be called the "successor."

This simplest and most common type of precedence relationship is called a "finish-to-start" or "FS" relationship. Other more complex types of precedence relationships exist, such as "start-to-start" and "finish-to-finish." Such relationships are supported by all the popular project management software tools. If you are interested, I explain those more complex types of relationships in Appendix B, but I strongly recommend that you use only finish-to-start relationships whenever possible, even if that requires you to break the activities into a little more detail.

Figure 7.2 shows a complete network diagram using only finish-to-start precedence relationships for a very small project. The logic of this diagram is that before any activity can start, all of its predecessor activities must be finished. For example, activity E cannot begin until both B and D are finished. Notice two things about the way this diagram is drawn:

1. Each arrow connects one predecessor to one successor. There are no splitting or merging arrows. For example,

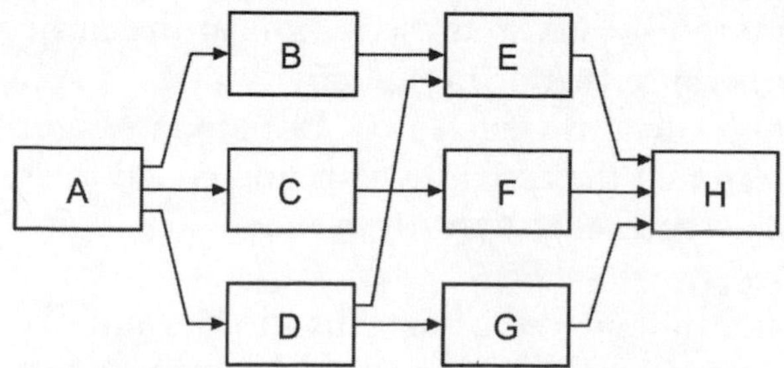

FIGURE 7.2 Example Network Diagram

the arrows from activity A to activities B, C, and D are three separate arrows, not an arrow that starts out as one arrow from A and then splits into three arrows. Similarly, the three arrows from activities E, F, and G do not merge to form one arrow to activity H. If you use splitting or merging arrows, then the meaning of intersecting arrows (such as the intersection between the arrow from C to F and the arrow from D to E) becomes ambiguous. The ambiguity is whether the arrows are intersecting logically or simply crossing. Is E preceded by B, C, and D, or is it preceded only by B and D. If you always follow the rule that each arrow connects only one predecessor to only one successor, you eliminate this ambiguity. Clearly, E is preceded only by B and D. Also, F is preceded only by C (not C and D). The two arrows are simply crossing, not intersecting logically.

2. Each arrow is clearly drawn from the right (finish) side of the predecessor node to the left (start) side of the successor node. These are clearly finish-to-start precedence relationships. If you draw the arrows any other way (for example, from or to the top of a node or the bottom of a node), the arrows may depict one of the other more complex types of precedence relationships (such as start-to-start), or their meaning may become totally unclear.

Although time flows from left to right in a project network diagram, don't make the mistake of thinking of the network diagram as a time-scaled representation of the project. For example, just because two or more activity nodes happen to align vertically in the diagram (such as E, F, and G in Figure 7.2), that does not mean that the activities start and end at the same times. The diagram represents only the sequencing logic among the activities.

Figures 7.3a and 7.3b illustrate another important feature of network diagrams. When a project has two or more activities

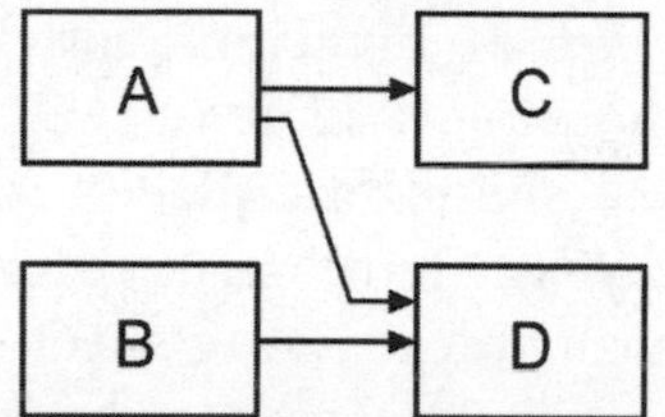

FIGURE 7.3a Network without Start and End Nodes

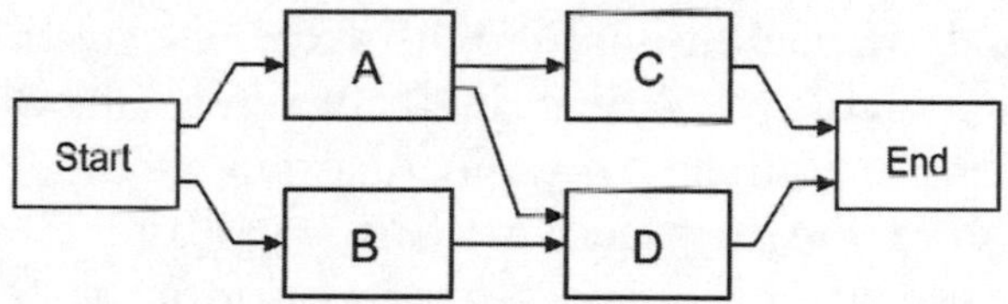

FIGURE 7.3b Network with Start and End Nodes Attached

that can begin immediately at the start of the project (activities A and B in Figure 7.3a), I recommend that you create an artificial (zero duration) "start" activity node and connect it with precedence relationships to the first real activities in the project as shown in Figure 7.3b. Similarly, if your network diagram ends with several activities that have no successors, I recommend that you create a dummy "end" node and connect all the final real activities to it with precedence relationships. In other words, your network diagram should have only one node with no predecessors and only one node with no successors. Most of the project management software tools refer to a zero-duration activity as a "milestone" and display the milestone as a diamond (rather than a bar) on the Gantt chart representation of the schedule.

The process of developing the network diagram involves a mental simulation of the project and is always best performed by the cross-functional team working together. The analysis proceeds from the beginning of the project to the end, and it goes like this. The team figures out which activities can start at the very beginning of the project; that is, which activities have no predecessors. Those activities are placed at the left end of the diagram. (I use a sticky note to represent each activity, so that it is easy to move them around on a long sheet of paper or a whiteboard as we build the diagram.) As soon as an activity node is placed in the network diagram, the team thinks of that activity as finished as far as their mental simulation is concerned. Then they ask, when all the activities that are already in the diagram have been finished, what additional activities can be started. As soon as they add an activity to the diagram, they figure out which of the activities that are already on the diagram would have to be finished before the new activity can start, and they draw in the precedence arrow from each predecessor to the new activity. This thought process is repeated until all the activities that appeared in the work breakdown structure have been placed into the network diagram. This process requires the team to visualize how the project will unfold and often causes them to discover activities that had been overlooked in the development of the WBS.

The project team should be aware that there are three different types of reasons for precedence relationships between activities in projects.

- **Technical Reason.** It is physically impossible to perform the activities in the opposite sequence or simultaneously. For example, it is impossible to test computer code before you develop the code. This type of reason accounts for the largest number of precedence relationships in most projects.
- **Policy/Preference Reason.** Although the activities could be performed in the opposite sequence or simultaneously, the team is required by policy or chooses to perform them in a certain sequence for some good reason. The underlying good reason often relates to quality, efficiency, speed,

safety, or security. For example, if you had to paint the ceiling and install carpet in a room, it is physically possible to perform those two activities in either order. But you would choose to paint the ceiling first. In this case, gravity is the good reason.

- **Restricted Resource.** Although the two activities could be performed simultaneously as far as technical and policy/preference considerations are concerned, the two activities both require exactly the same resource (for example, a given person or item of equipment), and that resource can be devoted to only one activity at a time.

The network diagram for the Melbourne Plant Development Project is displayed in Figure 7.4 on the following page. All of the activities identified in the work breakdown structure (Figure 6.3) show up in the diagram. Notice that the diagram has a "start" node at the very beginning, because both "Prepare Production Requirements Analysis" and "Select/Confirm Plant Manager" can start at the beginning of the project. There is no need for an artificial "end" node, because "Train Personnel" is the only activity with no successors.

If you read the "Project Narrative" in Figure 7.5 on page 91, you will see that the network diagram captures the sequencing requirements described in the narrative. Of course, you would not typically have a written project narrative, nor would you need to develop one, for a real project as this information resides in the experiences of your team members. However, the narrative illustrates the process of thinking through the project to develop the sequencing logic captured in the network diagram.

As I describe the remaining steps in the Project Success Method, you will see the tremendous value of the network diagram. It facilitates both the planning and control processes. Developing the project network diagram is definitely *the easier way*.

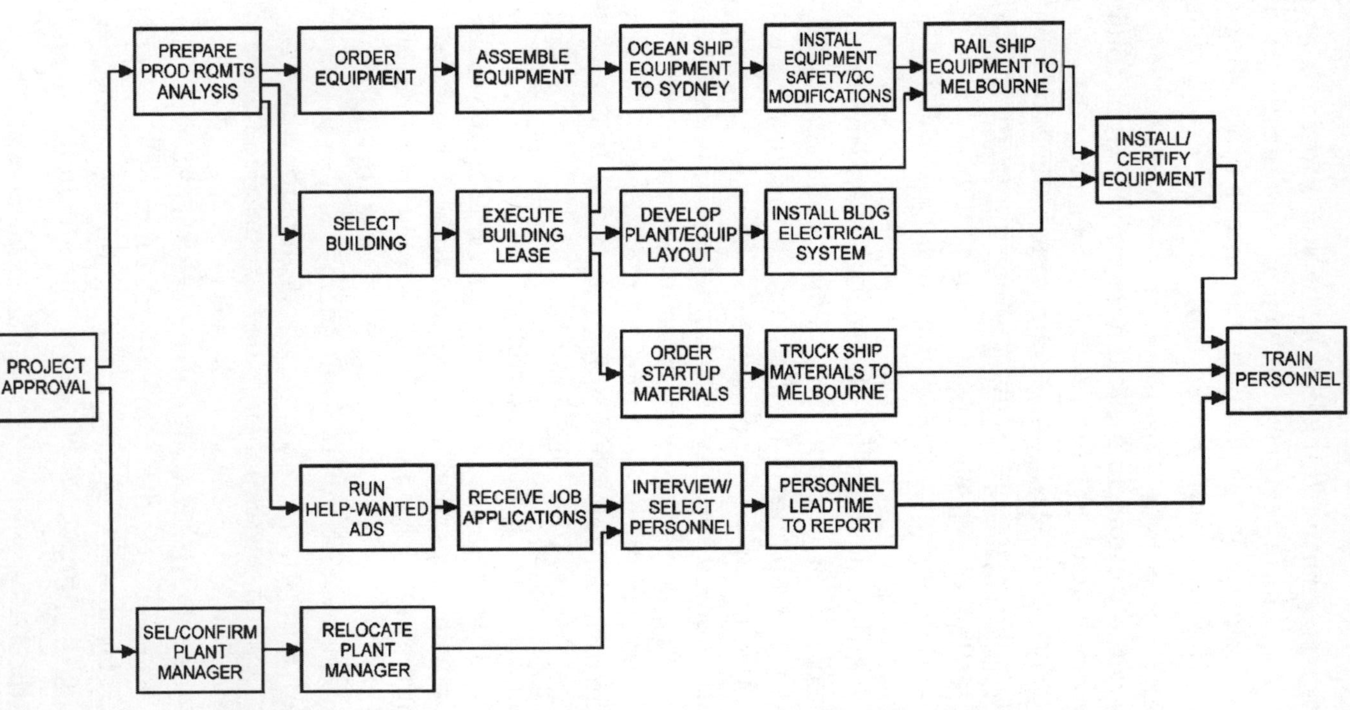

FIGURE 7.4 Network Diagram for Melbourne Plant Development Project

Melbourne Plant Development Project

Project Narrative

The Industrial Engineering staff will immediately prepare a "production requirements analysis," which determines the equipment required as well as the amounts of floor-space and personnel needed. Meanwhile, the VP-International Operations will immediately begin the process of selecting and confirming one of Century Manufacturing Company's veteran plant managers to manage the new plant.

As soon as the production requirements analysis is complete, a purchase order will be placed for the necessary equipment. As soon as the vendor receives CMC's purchase order, the assembly of the equipment will begin. The vendor will then ship the equipment by ocean freight to CMC's Regional Headquarters complex in Sydney. While the equipment is in Sydney, the Corporate Maintenance Department will install the standard CMC safety and quality control modifications.

The process of selecting a building to lease for the new plant can begin immediately after the production requirements analysis is complete. The International Legal staff will be responsible for ensuring that an acceptable lease is executed on the building after final selection. As soon as the lease has been executed, an Industrial Engineer will develop a plant/equipment layout. Then an approved contractor will install the electrical system in the building in preparation for the installation of the production equipment.

Once the building lease has been executed and the equipment safety and quality control modifications have been completed, the modified equipment will be shipped by rail from Sydney to the Melbourne Plant. However, final installation and certification of the equipment cannot begin until the electrical system has been installed in the building.

Purchase orders will be placed for the startup production materials after the building lease has been executed. The materials will be truck shipped from various Australian vendors directly to the new plant.

Based on the production requirements analysis, the Human Resources Department will run help-wanted ads in Melbourne area newspapers for operating personnel. The ads will specify a date by which job applications must be received.

FIGURE 7.5 Narrative Description of Melbourne Plant Development Project

Once selected, the manager of the new plant will relocate to Melbourne. After arriving in Melbourne, the Plant Manager will interview and select the operating personnel. All selected personnel will be required to report for work three weeks after the end of the selection period.

As soon as: (a) the operating personnel have reported, and (b) the equipment has been installed and certified, and (c) the materials have been delivered—the Corporate Trainer will train the operating personnel. When the training is finished, the project will be complete, and production operations can begin under the direction of the Plant Manager.

FIGURE 7.5 *(Continued)*

Key Takeaways

- Trying to maintain an up-to-date schedule for a strategic project is practically impossible, unless the schedule is based on a project network diagram.
- Have the project team work together cross-functionally to develop the network diagram.
- Developing the network diagram involves thinking through the project from beginning to end, adding the activity nodes and precedence arrows as you go through the mental simulation.
- There are three types of reasons for precedence relationships between activities.
- To ensure that the logic of the diagram is unambiguous, follow the formatting rules explained in this chapter.

8

Try to Be Normal

The next step in the planning process is to estimate the durations of the activities. This is the first point where we begin to quantify the plan, and it can make team members a little nervous. I will say more about that later in this chapter.

The activity durations for most strategic projects are estimated in working days. However, if you are planning a project in which most activities are performed in less than a day (such as an industrial maintenance project on which work continues 24 hours per day), you would estimate the durations in working hours. Notice that the question is how long it will take on the calendar or the clock to get the activity done, *not* how many staff-hours of work will be involved.

Some activities continue during non-working days. An example is the curing of concrete. The concrete doesn't know or care whether or not a given day is a working day. For those types of activities, you just need to tell your project management software tool that the estimate is in calendar days rather than working days. The popular software tools allow you to define special calendars of working days versus non-working days for activities for which the typical five workdays per week calendar does not apply.

General Approach to Scheduling

Now let's take a look at the approach most people use to come up with their project schedule, and thus, the durations of their activities. Is this the approach you use?

Case Study: Mediterranean Pasta Delights

Mediterranean Pasta Delights is a chain of franchisee-owned and operated fast-food restaurants specializing in pasta dishes. The date of the annual franchisee conference has been announced. The four-day meeting with 1,500 participants will involve instructional sessions, executive updates, and a motivational speaker, as well as social and recreational activities. Salvatore Francona, project manager for the event, is talking with Annette Domingo, Director of Franchisee Relations.

"Sal, the franchisee conference has really sneaked up on us this year. I guess we were just too absorbed in the rollout of the new marketing program. How's your project team coming on preparations for the conference?" Annette asked.

"OK, I guess," Sal replied, "although I sure wish we had gotten an earlier start. We've developed a schedule for the project that meets the deadline date, but I don't think any of us feel very confident about it."

"How did you come up with the schedule?"

* This case is fictitious. Any similarity to actual, existing companies, individuals, or projects is purely coincidental.

"The only way I know how to develop a schedule for a project with a fixed deadline," he explained. "We started at the deadline and worked backward specifying when each activity would have to be finished. I guess you could say that we force-fitted the schedule. I hope it's not just 'pie in the sky.'"

Questions

1. For what specific reasons do you suppose Sal and his team members lack confidence in the project schedule?
2. What effects will the team's lack of confidence in the schedule likely have on their performance of the project?
3. Can you think of a better approach to developing a schedule for a project with a fixed deadline?

I refer to Sal's force-fitting approach as "back-scheduling from the deadline," and we see lots of people using it—but with little success. It seems logical, and you always get a schedule that meets the deadline. Unfortunately, the schedule almost never works, so the project runs late. Fortunately, The Project Success Method offers a better and easier way.

First, let's understand four problems you encounter when you use a back-scheduling or force-fitting approach.

1. The problem that is most obvious to the team members is that the approach simply allocates a certain amount of time for each activity without specifying how the activity will be performed in that amount of time. In fact, there's no evidence or assurance that it is even possible to perform each activity in the amount of time that's been allotted. To some extent, the process becomes a numbers game, with little connection to the real work to be done.
2. The second problem is a direct result of the first. Because the team members have serious doubts about the feasibility

of the activity durations, they are less inclined to commit to the schedule. They tend to regard the schedule as "pie in the sky" and to have a diminished sense of mutual accountability for executing work on schedule. In essence, they expect to run late!

3. It's quite likely that some activities have been compressed too much and others should be compressed more. As we will see in Chapter 10, activities that are good candidates for compression tend to have certain specific characteristics, while other activities should never be compressed. But, the back-scheduling approach generally treats all activities as equally good choices for compression. It seems fair to treat all activities the same.
4. The final problem may be the least obvious, but the most dangerous. The back-scheduling approach specifies the *latest allowable* time that each activity can be finished, rather than the *earliest possible* finish time. When every activity is scheduled to be completed at its latest allowable finish time, there is virtually no margin for slippage in any of the activities. In other words, there's no "slack" in the schedule. So the probability of actually completing the project by the deadline is small, even though the schedule meets the deadline, at least on paper.

A far more effective approach is "*forward scheduling and strategic compression*." It's the approach we use on every project that we help our clients plan. Here's how it works:

1. Develop the network diagram for the project, as explained in Chapter 7. This approach to scheduling cannot be used unless the schedule is based on a network diagram.
2. Estimate the "normal duration" for each activity, which is the duration associated with the lowest cost approach (not the fastest approach) to performing the activity. We will discuss in detail the thought process involved in estimating

normal durations later in this chapter. A key requirement of this approach to scheduling is that the team member responsible for managing each activity must have confidence in and be committed to the normal duration estimate for the activity.

3. Using the normal duration estimates in conjunction with the project network diagram, your project management software tool will perform scheduling calculations (as explained in Chapter 9) to determine the initial project duration and completion date. The initial completion date will typically be later than the deadline—often significantly later. The calculations also determine the initial critical path(s) of the project, which is/are the path(s) of activities driving the project duration.
4. Selectively compress one activity at a time until the project is compressed to the deadline or perhaps even to a date earlier than the deadline. This compression process is explained in Chapter 10, and it involves looking at the trade-offs between the costs of compressing the activities and the savings associated with shortening the project.

As you will see in Chapter 10, this "forward scheduling and strategic compression" approach to project scheduling avoids all four of the problems described above for the "back-scheduling" or "force-fitting" approach. And it still produces a schedule the meets or even beats the project deadline. And even better, it can save you a ton of money!

The "Normal Duration"

Now let's return to the challenge of estimating the normal duration of each activity. First, we need to understand exactly what "normal duration" means. Figure 8.1 shows the general relationship between the planned duration of an activity and the

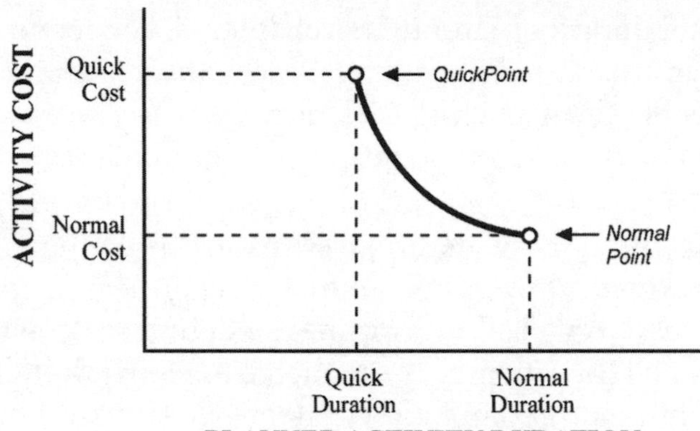

FIGURE 8.1 General Relationship Between Planned Activity Duration and Activity Cost

cost (labor, materials, etc.) of performing that activity. There is some most cost-efficient way of performing the activity, which is called the "normal point" in the relationship. Associated with that point are the normal duration and the normal (minimum possible) cost. For most activities, it is possible to shorten the duration, if you are willing to spend more money (for overtime, additional workers or equipment, a contractor, etc.) on the activity In general, the more you compress the duration, the more expensive it becomes to compress it farther, until you reach the point of minimum duration. Many people refer to the point of minimum duration as the "crash point," but we work with clients in both the aerospace and software industries, who object strongly to the word "crash." So I refer to the point of minimum duration as the "quick point." Associated with that point are the quick (minimum) duration and the quick cost.

Sometimes when I am teaching the Project Success Method, a participant in the class will say something like, "I understand the concept of the normal point, but at my company, we are under so much pressure to get our projects done as fast as possible that we just go ahead and estimate the quick durations for all our activities." In other words, they minimize duration rather than cost for all activities. Other participants in the class will often nod in agreement. It's a macho-sounding thing to say, but nobody actually plans projects with all the activities at their minimum possible durations. And if they did, it would be incredibly stupid! Why would you want to compress any activity from its normal duration until you have determined (1) that your project duration needs to be compressed, (2) that compressing the activity in question will actually shorten the project duration, and (3) that it is the best activity to compress among all the activities that are driving the project duration? Until you know that all three of these statements are true, you could be compressing an activity that should not be compressed. You would be driving up the cost of your project, increasing the stress on your project team, and possibly endangering project quality and/or safety, while gaining nothing in return!

The Estimating Process

When you or one of your team members estimates the normal duration of an activity, the following seven-step mental process will usually lead to a good estimate:

1. What is the scope of this activity, and what are the quality expectations? Here's a little story I love that illustrates the point perfectly.

> Bubba loved to fish, and he loved all types of fishing. But he had never been ice fishing, because he lived in Florida. Finally one winter, he spent some vacation time up north and had his first opportunity to go ice fishing. When he got home, his Florida fishing buddies, who had never been ice fishing either, were interested to hear all about his ice fishing experience.
>
> "Did you enjoy it?" they asked.

"No," Bubba responded, "To tell you the truth, it's the only kind of fishing I have ever done that I didn't enjoy."

"Why not?" asked Bubba's friends. "Was it too cold?"

"I don't even remember how cold it was," Bubba said. "It was just so darn much work. It took half a day to cut a hole in the ice big enough to put the boat in!"

So before you try to estimate how long it will take to cut a hole in the ice, you need to know how big the hole really needs to be.

2. What technological approach will be used to perform this activity? Again, when estimating a normal duration, the technological approach should be the most cost-efficient way to perform the work. Should Bubba use an ice pick, an ax, a keyhole saw, a chain saw, an auger, or some other technology to cut the hole in the ice?
3. What specific resources (people, equipment, contractors, etc.) will be used to perform this activity? The answer to this question can affect the answers to the next two questions.
4. What is the work effort (typically measured in staff-hours) of this activity?
5. Considering all the pre-existing commitments of the required resources to other project and non-project work, what is the average availability (typically measured as a percentage of work time or in staff-hours/workday) of the resources to work on this activity?
6. Given the answers to the above questions, how many workdays will be required to perform this activity, assuming no problems?
7. Should the duration estimate be adjusted upward to account for the average impact of common problems and uncontrollable factors that can interrupt or delay this activity (such as inclement weather, personnel absences, equipment breakdowns, etc.)? This is a risk-management technique. We want an estimate that reflects the conditions of the real

world—not an estimate that assumes a perfect world that always cooperates.

Here's an example. Suppose you are estimating the duration of an activity that will be performed by two specific people, both of whom work 8 hours per day, 5 days per week. Based on the scope of the activity, the technological approach being used, and the skill level of the people who will do the work, you estimate that the activity involves about 40 staff-hours of work. Because the two resource people are also involved in other activities and other projects, as well as non-project work (which some people refer to as their "day job"), you estimate that they will be available only about 25 percent of their time to work on the activity. That's 2 staff-hours available per day for each of two people or a total of 4 staff-hours per day. So it should take 10 working days to perform the 40 staff-hours of work. But suppose you also believe that common problems and other uncontrollable factors are likely to delay this activity by an average of 20 percent. So you would adjust the duration estimate up from 10 to 12 working days.

Please understand I am not suggesting here that you need to go through a detailed analysis of the type I have just illustrated for every activity. However, I am suggesting that the factors illustrated in the example should be taken into consideration in your mental estimating process.

By far, the best source of the normal duration estimate for a given activity is the team member responsible for managing that activity. Sometimes, the activity manager will need to consult some other source of information to come up with the estimate. For example, if the activity manager will not actually perform the activity, he or she will probably need to check with the resource(s) that will perform the activity. The resources could be internal personnel or external vendors, contractors, approval authorities, etc. The activity manager may need to look at historical records of the actual durations of similar activities in previous projects or consult a colleague who has managed this type of activity in previous projects.

Now let's take a look at an all too common and highly dysfunctional approach to involving team members in the duration estimating process.

Case Study: GMB Pharmaceuticals

GMB Pharmaceuticals is undertaking an employee job satisfaction study. Michael O'Brien from the Human Resources Department is the project manager for the study, which will gather and analyze data on approximately 3,500 employees. Michael is leading the team through the project planning process and is currently asking each team member to estimate the normal duration of each activity that he or she is responsible for managing. Shannon Murphy from the Research Department is a statistician on the project team.

"Shannon, what's your estimate of the normal duration for the activity 'Analyze Survey Data'?" Michael asked.

"I have no idea, Mike. It depends on too many things that I have no control over," Shannon said.

"I understand that there's uncertainty about all these duration estimates, but I need your best guess. Otherwise, we won't be able to develop a project schedule. Just give me a duration that you feel comfortable with," he said.

"Well, OK then," she said and paused to think. "I guess I'd be comfortable with a duration of two weeks or ten working days."

"Two weeks! Come on, Shannon. Why so long?" Michael asked. "You've got a computer, don't you? I mean it's not like you'll be doing the analysis on an abacus."

"There's more to it than crunching numbers with the computer, Mike, at least if you really want to learn something useful from this survey. Besides, I'm thinking about all

* This case is fictitious. Any similarity to actual, existing companies, individuals, or projects is purely coincidental.

the other projects I'm involved in right now, including some product R&D projects, which frankly take priority over this study. I'm just not sure I can commit to anything less than ten days on this activity," she replied.

"We're all busy, Shannon. Look, I think five working days should be more than long enough for this activity. How about if we use five days as the duration estimate?" Michael asked.

"Use whatever you like," Shannon said. "It's your schedule—not mine. And by the way, Mike, why did you ask me for the duration estimate in the first place?"

Questions

1. What problems has Mike probably created as a result of his handling of this situation?
2. How long do you think Shannon's activity will actually take?
3. If Mike could have this conversation over again, what changes would you recommend in his approach?

Mike started out well, but then he made a classic mistake that could haunt him in ways that go way beyond the activity in question. Mike deserves credit for asking the activity manager to estimate the activity duration, for explicitly recognizing the uncertainty associated with the estimating process, and for suggesting that the activity manager give an estimate with which she was comfortable.

Mike blew it, however, when he questioned Shannon's duration estimate as being too long, insinuated that Shannon was not giving her best effort, and arbitrarily cut her estimate. Mike's mistake was to place more emphasis on the duration estimate than on the activity manager's *commitment* to the estimate.

This mistake can have far-reaching damaging effects on Mike's efforts as a project manager. First, Mike has lost Shannon's commitment to the duration estimate for this activity, as well as any other activities that she is responsible for managing on this project. She might even, consciously or unconsciously, drag out her activities on this project in retaliation for the way she's been treated and to prove that her duration estimate was correct in the first place—the "I told you so" phenomenon.

Her negative attitude toward Mike also is likely to carry over to any future projects in which she is a team member and Mike is the project manager. Shannon will probably think that if Mike doesn't like any other estimate she gives him, he will arbitrarily cut it back. So in the future, she will inflate her estimates even more, so that when he cuts them back, she'll still have a reasonable amount of time to get the work done. Mike has kicked off what we call "the escalating estimate padding and slashing game," and mutual trust is the first casualty.

Perhaps more important, Shannon is not the only person affected by this conversation. All the team members in the meeting also heard Mike, and their reactions would probably be similar to Shannon's. So Mike's mistake is likely to have a serious negative impact, not only on Shannon's commitment, but on all the team members' commitment to the project plan, and to the project management process. Mike just destroyed the mutual accountability and support associated with a real team. The effects of Mike's mistake could well follow him when he manages future projects. Mike's error could even contribute to a negative general attitude toward project management in the organization as a whole.

When you ask a team member to estimate the duration of an activity that they are responsible for managing, you want two things—*the duration estimate* and *the team member's commitment* to do everything within his or her power to deliver the activity in the estimated amount of time. Of the two, the commitment is far more important than the estimate itself. Without the commitment, the duration estimate has no real value. It's just a number that you can plug into your plan, but there's no reason to have confidence in that number. If you get the commitment, however, the magnitude of the estimate may not be very important, and here's why.

When you put the estimate into the project network diagram and perform the scheduling calculations, one of the following will happen:

- The calculated project completion date is acceptable, or,
- The calculated project completion date is unacceptably late, but the activity in question is not on the critical path; that is, the sequence of activities that is driving the completion date, or,
- The calculated project completion date is unacceptably late, and the activity in question is on the critical path.

Only in the third case would you have reason to be concerned about the duration estimate for the activity. In that case, you would be able to go back to the activity manager (in the schedule compression process described in Chapter 10) and ask the activity manager whether compressing the activity would be possible. If so, how could it be done, how much could the duration be compressed without causing problems, and how much would it cost? In our experience, many activity managers will voluntarily compress their activity at no cost, saying something like, "Now that I see the activity is on the critical path, I'll do what it takes to get it done in only five days." In other cases, the activity manager may suggest an approach to compressing the activity that will increase the cost of the activity (such as using overtime labor), or he or she may insist that the activity cannot be compressed. Regardless of the outcome of the inquiry, you will not have lost the commitment and trust of that team member or other team members. Again, **without the team's commitment, your project schedule is pure fantasy!**

Potential Issues in Duration Estimating

Over the years, I have noticed several issues that sometimes arise in the process of estimating the normal durations of the activities.

First, although most project managers worry about the possibility that team members will "pad" their estimates, my experience indicates that activity managers tend to grossly underestimate their durations. The reasons they underestimate the duration are that:

- They fail to recognize the full scope of the activity (step 1 in the seven-step estimating process), and/or
- They fail to consider that the people who will perform the activity will not be available to work on the activity full-time (step 5), and/or
- They fail to consider common problems and uncontrollable factors that can slow down or interrupt the activity (step 7).

So although I would rarely recommend that you challenge an estimate as being too long, I often challenge estimates that I think are too short for one of those reasons.

Another problem has to do with the potential confusion between activity work effort versus activity duration. Suppose you ask an activity manager for a duration estimate, and the activity manager says, "That activity will take about 40 hours." You should not assume that the activity will take 5 working days of 8 hours per day. The activity manager is probably referring to 40 staff-hours of work, and as we saw in the example earlier in this chapter, an activity involving 40 staff-hours of work could easily take more (or less) than 5 working days to perform. So always ask, "How many working days will you need to get the activity done?"

A third problem has to do with potential confusion between working days versus calendar days. Suppose you ask an activity manager for a duration estimate, and the activity manager says, "Give me about 30 days to get it done." Whenever the estimate is

30 days (or an even multiple of 30 days), I always ask, "Do you mean 30 working days or do you mean you need about a month?" If you put 30 into the project management software tool as the duration estimate, the tool will interpret it as 30 working days or six weeks. If, on the other hand, the activity manager meant that he or she needs about a month, the duration estimate you should enter into the software tool is about 21 working days.

The last problem is something I mentioned at the very beginning of this chapter. Some team members will get nervous when the project manager asks for a duration estimate. They realize that they are being asked to commit to their estimate, but they don't know the "correct answer;" that is, the accurate estimate. Trust me; nobody knows the "correct" duration estimate for the vast majority of activities. The best we can do is make a reasonable guess, so that we can move ahead with the planning process. I encourage project managers to put their team members at ease by explicitly mentioning the unavoidable uncertainty in the estimating process and encouraging activity managers to provide estimates with which they are comfortable. To the extent that some of the estimates may be too high, they will probably be offset by others that are too low. And remember, some of the duration estimates will change later in the planning process anyway. I usually say something like, "Rather than worrying about the 'inaccuracies' of your duration estimates, you should be worried about the activities that you haven't even identified yet."

Activity Durations for the Melbourne Plant Development Project

Figure 8.2 shows the normal duration estimates for the Melbourne Plant Development Project. To review some of the points made earlier in this chapter, let me point out a few things about the durations shown.

First, notice how many of the duration estimates are multiples of 5 working days. This is quite typical. Activity managers

Melbourne Plant Development Project
Normal Duration Estimates

Activity	Working Days
Prepare Production Requirements Analysis	3
Order Equipment	3
Assemble Equipment	20
Ocean Ship Equipment to Sydney	40
Install Equipment Safety/QC Modifications	10
Rail Ship Equipment to Melbourne Plant	5
Install/Certify Equipment	5
Select Building	30
Execute Building Lease	10
Develop Plant/Equipment Layout	5
Install Building Electrical System	10
Order Startup Materials	3
Truck Ship Materials to Melbourne Plant	10
Select/Confirm Plant Manager	5
Relocate Plant Manager	30
Run Help-Wanted Ads	10
Receive Job Applications	10
Interview/Select Personnel	10
Personnel Leadtime to Report	15
Train Personnel	10

FIGURE 8.2 **Normal Duration Estimates for Melbourne Plant Development Project**

often estimate in weeks and then convert the estimates to working days. No problem with that approach. Also, notice that 16 of the 20 durations are within the "sweet spot" (3 to 15 working days) that I mentioned in Chapter 6.

Second, the scope of each activity is considered in estimating its normal duration. I remember when we were planning the real project on which this case is based. We asked the executive who was responsible for "Select/Confirm Plant Manager" to estimate the duration of that activity, and he said, "Oh, I can do that in 5 minutes." He was thinking about how long it take him to decide which of his veteran plant managers he would like to send to Melbourne. In fact, I suspect that he had already made that decision. However, the scope of the activity includes negotiating with the selected person to confirm the selection. And if the negotiations are not successful, it will be necessary to go to the second choice, and so on. After discussing the scope of the activity, the activity manager changed his estimate to 5 working days.

Next, the estimates take into consideration that the resources who will be performing each activity may have other project and non-project duties that will limit their availability to work on the activity. So for example, the estimate of 3 days for "Order Equipment" does not mean that it will take a person 3 days working full time to order the equipment. Rather, it means that we are allowing 3 days to get the activity done after the predecessor activity (Prepare Production Requirements Analysis) is finished.

Finally, some of the activities, especially "Assemble Equipment" and "Install Building Electrical System," will be performed by resources (a vendor and a contractor) that are external to Century Manufacturing Company. The activity manager for each of those activities would certainly need to consult with the external resource to come up with the duration estimate for the activity. Also, notice that from the external resource's point of view, "Assemble Equipment" and "Install Building Electrical System" are actually projects in themselves, although we are treating them as activities within the plant development project.

Key Takeaways

- Never force-fit a project schedule by back-scheduling from the deadline. Instead, use the forward scheduling and strategic compression approach to develop a project schedule that meets or beats the deadline.

- For each activity, estimate the normal duration; that is, the duration if the activity is performed in the most cost-efficient way.
- Encourage team members to use the seven-step thought process presented in this chapter for estimating normal activity durations. The estimates should take into consideration the scope of the activity, the technological approach to performing the work, the availability of the resources, and common problems/factors that could slow down or interrupt the work.
- Seek commitment to duration estimates. The commitment is far more important than the estimate itself, especially at this stage in the planning process. Never challenge a duration estimate as being too long.
- Calm the nervousness of team members about the uncertainties in estimating their activity durations by encouraging them to estimate durations with which they are comfortable.
- Be aware of the tendency for activity managers to grossly underestimate normal activity durations.

9

Figure Out What's Critical

Once the project team has developed the project network diagram and estimated the normal activity durations, it is ready to perform the scheduling calculations to determine the initial project duration and the initial critical path(s). This is the point in the methodology where the software tool finally starts to work. The software tool will make these calculations quickly and correctly as often as necessary, during both the planning and control phases of the project.

In this chapter, I will explain only the "forward pass" calculations that determine the earliest possible starting time and the earliest possible completion time for each activity. That information allows you to determine the initial project duration and the initial critical path(s). If you are interested in the other scheduling calculations, including the calculation and interpretation of "slack" values, I provide a complete explanation in Appendix C.

The easiest way to understand the forward pass scheduling calculations is to look at an example. Figure 9.1 shows an

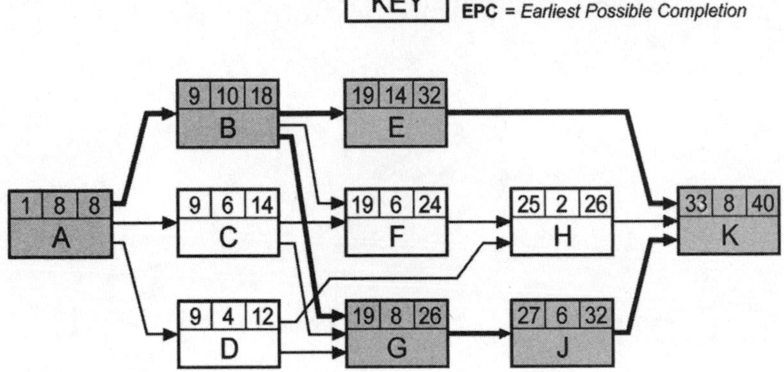

FIGURE 9.1 **Example of Forward Pass Schedule Calculations**

example for which the forward pass calculations have already been made. As indicated in the key, the activity durations (DUR) are shown in the top center boxes within the activity nodes. I will assume that the durations are expressed in working days. The earliest possible starting times (EPS) are shown in the boxes at the upper left of each node, and the earliest possible completion times (EPC) are shown in the boxes at the upper right.

First, we would specify the starting date of the project or the EPS for activity A. We will treat the project starting date as day 1 of the project for the purposes of these calculations. If activity A starts on day 1 and has a duration of 8 working days, it should be completed on working day 8.

Since activity A is the only predecessor to B, activity B can begin on the working day following the completion of A. So B can start on day 9. If B begins on day 9 and takes 10 days, it should end on day 18.

Now we must work in columns of activities as we move across the network diagram. In general, we cannot perform all the calculations for an entire path (such as A-B-E-K) to the end of the project.

So we go next to activity C. Since A is the only predecessor to C, activity C can also start on working day 9. And since the duration of C is 6 working days, C should be completed on day 14.

Similarly, we calculate the EPS and EPC values for activities D and E as shown in Figure 9.1.

When we get to activity F, we encounter the first case where there is more than one predecessor activity. Activity F cannot start until *both* B and C are completed. Although C should finish on day 14, B should not finish until day 18. Since B will finish later than C, activity B drives the earliest possible starting time for F, which is day 19. If F starts on day 19 and takes 6 days, it will be completed on day 24.

Activity G has three predecessors. Again, B has the latest EPC of the three predecessors, so it drives the EPS for G. And so on.

We just continue to follow this logic all the way to the end of the project. We determine that the EPC for the last activity (K) is 40, so the initial project duration is 40 working days. That project duration was not obvious when we started the calculations, but wasn't it easy to figure out? And what made it so easy? The network diagram is what made it so easy!

Of course, your project management software tool would convert the EPS and EPC values from workday numbers to calendar dates.

Now suppose you discovered another activity that you needed to add to the project plan. Do you see how easy it would be to insert the new activity node into the network diagram, connect it to the other activity nodes with precedence arrows as appropriate, and recalculate? What a piece of cake!

Before moving on to the discussion of critical paths, please notice that the network diagram in Figure 9.1 contained only finish-to-start relationships with no lags. If the network had contained more complex types of precedence relationships (as explained in Appendix B), the calculation procedures would have been much more complex.

There is another factor that would also make the calculation procedure more complex. If you enter into your project management software tool date constraints on the start or completion of activities within the network (for example, if you told the software tool that activity F cannot start before day 28 for some reason), then the calculation procedures would have been more complex.

The popular project management software tools can certainly handle the more complex calculations, but the results of the calculations are more difficult to interpret.

Defining and Finding Critical Path(s)

Now we have all the information we need to determine the location(s) of the critical path(s). A **critical path** is a connected sequence of activities from the beginning to the end of the project with the longest total duration of any path of activities through the project. A project can have more than one critical path. Because critical paths have the longest total duration, they drive the duration and completion date of the project.

Unfortunately, some of the popular project management tools identify critical path(s) incorrectly in my opinion. I explain the error that these tools make in Appendix C. The error is not fatal, in that it will not cause your project to fail, but it does sometimes confuse users of those software tools and cause them to doubt their understanding of "critical path."

Here is the foolproof method for finding your critical path (s). Start at the end of the project, and focus on the earliest possible starting time (EPS) for the last activity node in the network diagram. In Figure 9.1, the EPS for activity K is 33. Now ask, where did this EPC value come from? What predecessor(s) drove this EPS to be 33? In other words, what predecessor (s) had an EPC of 32? In this case, activities E and J (but not H) had an EPC of 32. So we have at least two critical paths—one coming through activity E and the other coming through activity J. We need to trace both paths back to the start of the project, and as we do, they could split again.

Following the path that led to activity E, the EPS for E (19) was obviously driven by B (its only predecessor), and the EPS of B (9) was driven by A. So one critical path contains the activities *A-B-E-K*. If that path is a critical path, the total duration of the path must be 40 working days, and it is.

Following the path that led to activity J, the EPS for J (27) was driven by G. The EPS of G (19) was driven by B (not C or D), and the EPS of B (9) was driven by A. So the second critical path is *A-B-G-J-K*, and the total duration of that path is also 40 working days.

So we have two critical paths. Again, the critical paths were not obvious before we performed the calculations, but they were easy to identify because of the network diagram.

Now that we know the definition of "critical path" and how to find the critical path(s) in a project, you might reasonably ask, "Who cares? Why do I need to know the location(s) of the critical path(s) in my project?" There are two important reasons—one of which relates to the project planning process and the second of which relates to the project control process.

1. The reason that relates to project planning is that to compress the duration of your project, you must compress all critical paths.
2. The reason that relates to project control is that any schedule slippage along *any* critical path will delay project completion.

So knowing the critical path(s) of a project is essential to making good project management decisions with respect to the time dimension of project performance. And remember, the management of the time dimension of project performance is the key to overall project success.

Don't think of the critical path(s) of a project as being static. The critical path(s) is/are likely to change, both as you plan and compress the project, and as you execute and control the project. For example, if you compressed the duration of activity B from 10 to 5 working days, the critical path would shift. Instead of the two critical paths running through B, there would be only one critical path running through C (the path A-C-G-J-K). Similarly, if activity C fell behind schedule and took 11 days, the critical path would shift in the same way. Because these types of changes occur frequently over the life of a project, we update the calculations often to determine how the schedule, and especially the project duration and critical path(s) have changed. Thank goodness for the project management software tool!

As I mentioned earlier with respect to the calculations, the identification of the critical path(s) would also be more complex if the network diagram contained precedence relationships other than finish-to-start with no lags.

Scheduling Calculations and Critical Path for the Melbourne Plant Development Project

Figure 9.2 shows the forward pass scheduling calculations for the Melbourne Plant Development Project based on the normal activity durations. The initial project duration is 96 working days, which is significantly longer than the limit of 70 working days as specified in the project charter (Figure 5.1). This outcome is typical of real projects. We often see situations in which the initial project duration is more than twice the allowable duration. But don't worry. In the next chapter, we will figure out how to compress the project to meet or beat the deadline and we will do so without losing the team's commitment to the schedule.

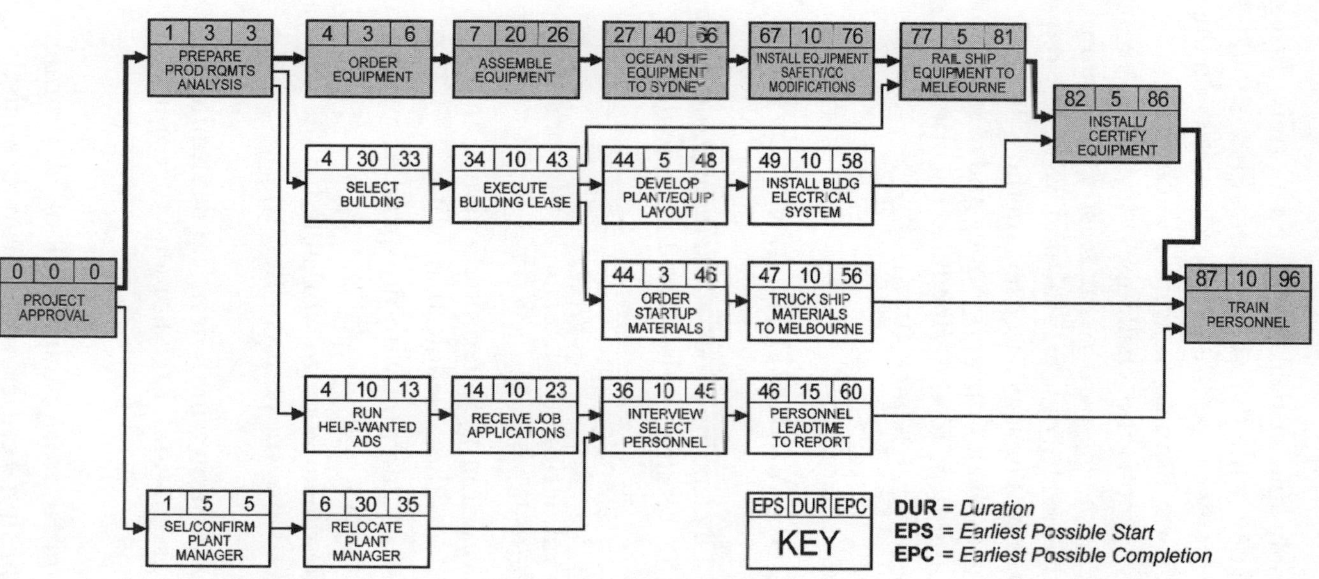
0 0 0
PROJECT APPROVAL
1 3 3
PREPARE PROD RQMTS ANALYSIS
4 3 6
ORDER EQUIPMENT
7 20 26
ASSEMBLE EQUIPMENT
27 40 66
OCEAN SHIP EQUIPMENT TO SYDNEY
67 10 76
INSTALL EQUIPMENT SAFETY/CC MODIFICATIONS
77 5 81
RAIL SHIP EQUIPMENT TO MELBOURNE
82 5 86
INSTALL/ CERTIFY EQUIPMENT
4 30 33
SELECT BUILDING
34 10 43
EXECUTE BUILDING LEASE
44 5 48
DEVELOP PLANT/EQUIP LAYOUT
49 10 58
INSTALL BLDG ELECTRICAL SYSTEM
44 3 46
ORDER STARTUP MATERIALS
47 10 56
TRUCK SHIP MATERIALS TO MELBOURNE
87 10 96
TRAIN PERSONNEL
4 10 13
RUN HELP-WANTED ADS
14 10 23
RECEIVE JOB APPLICATIONS
36 10 45
INTERVIEW SELECT PERSONNEL
46 15 60
PERSONNEL LEADTIME TO REPORT
1 5 5
SEL/CONFIRM PLANT MANAGER
6 30 35
RELOCATE PLANT MANAGER
EPS DUR EPC
KEY
DUR = Duration
EPS = Earliest Possible Start
EPC = Earliest Possible Completion

FIGURE 9.2 Initial Calculations for Melbourne Plant Development Project

There is only one critical path, and it runs through the activities associated with the equipment. That should not be surprising to you, since there are so many activities on the equipment path, and some of them have long durations.

So now we know the challenge we face. We need to compress the equipment path by at least 26 days. But as we do so, other paths may become critical, and we will be required to compress them, too. The key is to use a method that keeps track of the trade-offs between time and money and that does not lose the team's commitment to the schedule. I will explain how to meet this challenge in Chapter 10.

Schedule Validation and Revision

At this point in the planning process, the team should take a good hard look at the results of the schedule calculations in two respects:

1. **Schedule validation** to determine whether the schedule results seem valid, and
2. **Schedule revision** to determine whether any adjustments can be made to the schedule that will:
   a. compress its duration without spending money to compress activities, and/or
   b. make the schedule more workable for the team and the resources who will perform the work.

Schedule validation comes first. To determine whether the schedule results seem valid, I recommend that you ask two more specific questions:

1. Does the initial project duration look about right?
2. Does/do the initial critical path(s) run through the activities that I would expect to be on the critical path(s)?

You have intuition about your projects, and the more you use The Project Success Method, the more valid your intuition will become. Trust your intuition. If the schedule results don't look right to you, then something is probably wrong, and you need to find it and fix it before you move on to the next step.

Suppose you were planning the construction of a four-bedroom house using normal activity durations, and at this point in the planning process the schedule calculations are telling you that the project duration will be 20 working days, and that the critical path does not run through the excavation, foundation, framing, roofing, or drywall activities. The critical path does, however, run through an activity called "Install Mailbox." Even if you have no construction experience, you probably have enough intuition to know that these results cannot possibly be correct. So what could be wrong? Here are some things to check:

- **Missing activities.** The activities that are most likely to be overlooked are those that involve waiting rather than doing work from the team's perspective, such as waiting for concrete to cure or for materials to be delivered. If you discover a previously overlooked activity, you should add it to the work breakdown structure, assign an activity manager, insert it into the network diagram, and estimate its normal duration.
- **Incorrect project network diagram.** Repeat the mental simulation that you went through to develop the network diagram to be sure you captured the precedence relationships correctly. Maybe your network diagram shows that you can start installing the roof deck before you frame the house!

  Duration estimating errors, such as:
  - Estimating the quick duration rather than the normal duration
  - Failing to recognize the full scope of activities
  - Assuming full-time resource availability
  - Confusing working days and calendar days

  - Failing to recognize the expected impact of common problems and uncontrollable factors that could slow down or interrupt activities.
- **Data entry errors** (precedence relationships and/or durations).

Now let's look at schedule revision. Again, one purpose of schedule revision is to compress the project duration without spending any money to compress activity durations from their normal durations. The most common way to accomplish that is to find creative ways to make the precedence logic along the critical path(s) more aggressive. In the Melbourne Plant Development Project, for example, you may recall that the production requirements analysis tells us exactly what equipment we need to order. But we may know that any new plant will require at least one unit each of several standard items of equipment. So we could go ahead and order that standard set of equipment while the production requirements analysis is being performed. This would give the equipment vendor a head start on assembling the equipment. Then we would order the remaining equipment after we know the results of the production requirements analysis. This could shorten the critical path by several days, and it would not cost a dime! Appendix B shows how to split activities and modify the network diagram to accomplish more aggressive precedence logic.

The other purpose of schedule revision is to make the schedule more workable. The best way to find opportunities to make the schedule more workable is to distribute the schedule to all the team members and ask them to review it and speak up if they see any problems with executing the project according to the schedule. Here are two examples from real projects:

1. A company headquartered in Atlanta was developing a new IT application. One of the activities required a team member to travel to California to teach a two-day user training program on the new application for personnel in the Los

Angeles office. The schedule showed that the first day of the training program would be conducted on the Wednesday before Thanksgiving, and the second day would be taught on the following Monday. Of course, it was the team member responsible for that activity who spotted the problem and recognized the absurdity of the schedule for the activity. The scheduled was revised to have the training program start on the Monday following the four-day Thanksgiving holiday weekend.

2. A nonprofit service organization was planning a major fundraising event to be held on Valentine's Day. Most of the project team members were volunteers. The schedule showed lots of activities being performed during the last three weeks of December, when most of the team members would be unavailable due to their involvement in holiday season and other end-of-year activities. The project calendar was revised to treat the last three weeks of December as non-working days as far as the project was concerned.

I cannot provide an exhaustive list of problems that can arise or solutions that can be found with respect to the workability of a project schedule. Experience is the best teacher here. The key learning point and recommendation is to ask the team to review the project schedule for any problems associated with the activities for which they are responsible.

Key Takeaways

- The forward pass scheduling calculations determine the earliest possible start and completion times for each activity, the project duration, and the location(s) of the critical path(s).
- The critical path is the longest path through the project in terms of total duration, so the critical path drives the project duration. A project can have more than one critical path.

- A foolproof technique for finding the critical path(s) in a project involves tracing back the earliest possible starting times of the activities from the end of the project to the beginning.
- Knowing the location(s) of your critical path(s) is essential to making good project management decisions.
- The critical path(s) will probably change as you plan and as you control the project.
- Schedule validation involves applying your intuition to determine if the schedule looks correct with respect to project duration and critical path(s), and if not, finding and fixing the problem.
- Schedule revision involves using creativity to find ways to compress the project duration without spending money to compress activities or to make the schedule more workable for the project team and other resources involved in the project.

10

Compress for Profit

Remember that I call the schedule approach I am recommending and illustrating here "forward scheduling and strategic compression." In Chapters 8 and 9, we completed the forward scheduling by estimating the normal durations of the activities and performing the forward pass scheduling calculations. In the Melbourne Plant Development Project, we ended up with a completion date (working day 96) that was much later than the project deadline (working day 70), which is the typical result. Now we need to compress the project to meet or beat the project deadline. In my opinion, this is the most strategic step in the project planning process. If you are going to save money using The Project Success Method, this is the step where you will save the most money, and the potential exists to save huge amounts of money.

The Trade-Off Concept: Time versus Cost

Before I get into the compression process itself, let me explain the key trade-off concept that underlies this planning step. In

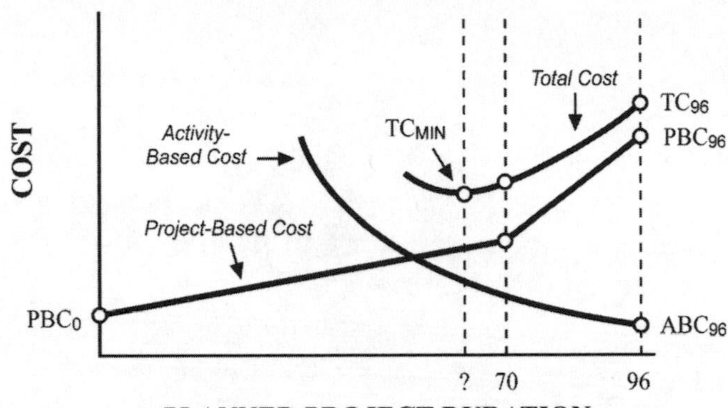

FIGURE 10.1 Time/Cost Trade-Off for Melbourne Plant Development Project

Chapter 8 (especially Figure 8.1), we looked at the relationship between the planned duration of an activity and the cost of performing the activity. We saw that the activity cost increased as we compressed the activity from its normal (most cost-efficient) point to its quick (shortest duration) point. Now I would like to raise that concept from the activity level to the project level as shown in Figure 10.1 for the Melbourne Plant Development Project. To understand the relationship, we need to recognize the two types of cost involved in projects.

First, we have the **activity-based costs**. Activity-based costs are the costs incurred in the performance of the activities, including labor, materials, leased special-purpose equipment such as a concrete pump, vendor or contractor fees, etc. These are exactly the same costs as were referenced in Figure 8.1 for the individual activities. The acid test of whether a given cost is an activity-based cost is to ask, "If the activity went away, would the cost go away?" If the answer to that question is yes, the cost is an activity-based cost.

We start our analysis at the initial project duration (96 working days), so the starting value of the activity-based costs is the sum of the normal costs for all the activities, which is the point labeled "ABC_{96}" at the project duration of 96 in Figure 10.1. The really good news is that we don't need to know what that number is to perform this analysis. In fact, we would not have developed a detailed budget yet. The key thing to understand is that since ABC_{96} is the sum of the normal costs for all the activities, it represents the minimum possible cost for performing all the activities in the project.

Now as we compress the project from its original 96-day duration, the activity-based cost begins to increase, because we are incurring the additional cost of compressing activities. At first, the activity-based cost rises fairly slowly as we pick the least expensive ways to compress the project. But the more we compress, the faster the activity-based cost increases, because (1) we are having to use more expensive ways to compress, and (2) we may be creating additional critical paths as we compress, and we must compress all critical paths in order to compress the project duration.

The other type of cost in all projects is the project-based costs. **Project-based costs** are costs incurred in the performance of the project that are not associated with the performance of any particular activity in the project. Project-based cost consists of *project overhead* (project management, leased general-purpose equipment such as a tower crane, interest on a project loan, etc.) and *opportunity cost*. Opportunity cost is the cost that is being incurred simply because the project is not finished and the expected payoff associated with the project is being lost over time. Opportunity costs can be huge. Examples include lost operating profit associated with (1) a new product or service that is not yet ready to be introduced to the market, (2) a new or renovated facility that is not yet ready to open, (3) incremental sales that will be generated by a marketing campaign that is not yet ready to launch, or (4) a production process that has been shut down for maintenance or repair. Another example is the lost operational savings associated with a new production process or management system that is not yet ready to be implemented. Customer-imposed penalties for late project completion and incentives for early completion are also included in this category.

Sometimes project-based cost is measured in something other than (or in addition to) dollars. We once had a group of people take the Project Success Method class who were working on the development of a program to educate women about the importance and the methods of early breast cancer detection. The most important project-based cost in their case was measured in lives! Assuming the program they were developing would be effective, every additional day that it took to complete the project could result in unnecessary deaths (of real people!) from breast cancer. They said they had never thought about it quite that way before.

Now let's return to Figure 10.1. Notice that the project-based cost starts at a value greater than zero (PBC_0) even for a project duration of zero. In other words, there is virtually always some fixed component of project-based cost—usually project start-up and shut-down costs—that do not vary with project duration. The other project-based costs, however, grow at a fairly constant rate as the project duration increases. When the project duration crosses the deadline (70 working days), the project-based cost suddenly begins to increase at a faster rate, as the strategic costs of late project completion kick in. So on the graph, the project-based cost at the initial project duration of 96 working days is the point PBC_{96}. As with ABC_{96}, we don't need to know the value of PBC_{96} in order to perform this analysis. We will be concerned only with the relative rates of change in the activity-based costs and the project-based costs.

Just another point of clarification before I move on. In Figure 10.1, the curves for the activity-based costs and the project-based costs intersect, but that is not important to this key trade-off concept. In real projects, they may or may not intersect. The activity-based cost (ABC_{96}) at the 96-day duration could be greater than the project-based costs (PBC_{96}), and the key trade-off concept would not change. Again, the shapes and relative slopes of the two curves are what really matter.

Of course, what we should be concerned about is total cost—that is, the sum of the activity-based costs and the project-based costs. Adding ABC_{96} and PBC_{96}, we get total cost at the initial duration of 96 days (TC_{96}).

Now here is the key trade-off concept. Suppose we compress the project duration by one day from 96 to 95. The activity-based cost will increase, because we have spent the money to compress an activity. But if we are smart in selecting the activity to compress, the activity-based cost will increase by a relatively small amount. However, the project-based cost will drop like a rock, as we shave one day off the project duration. In other words, the downward slope on the project-based cost line is much steeper than the upward slope on the activity-based cost curve as we move slightly to the left of the original project duration. So the total cost comes down. We are saving both time and money! This seems counterintuitive to some people, but it is absolutely true on virtually all strategic projects.

We continue compressing the project watching the trade-off between the increasing activity-based cost and the decreasing project-based cost. The total cost will continue to decrease as long as the project-based cost is decreasing faster than the activity-based cost is increasing.

Our first objective is to compress the project to the deadline as cost-efficiently as possible. Typically, total cost continues to decrease all the way until we reach the project deadline. But even it doesn't, we usually have to compress to the deadline anyway, and we will know that we have made good decisions in selecting the activities to compress every step of the way. It is quite common that even after we have compressed to the deadline, we find that we can continue to compress the project and total cost continues to decline as illustrated in Figure 10.1. In such cases, our second objective is to continue compressing until any further compression costs more than it is worth; that is, until the activity-based cost increase is greater than the project-based cost decrease for any further compression. We have reached the project duration associated with minimum total cost (TC_{MIN}).

That project duration is unknown until we perform the analysis, but it is fairly easy to figure out what it is.

The Compression Process

Compressing a project involves the steps explained below. It is crucially important that the project team members work together to perform these steps. That approach will lead to the best solution, and more important, it will maintain the team members' commitment to the compressed schedule.

Step 1: Estimate or Confirm the Late Penalty Rate and the Early Payoff Rate.

Remember that the late penalty rate is the additional *project-based* cost incurred for each workday that the project exceeds the deadline. It is the slope of the project-based cost line to the right of the deadline in Figure 10.1. That rate should have been estimated and included in the "Cost Expectations" section of the project charter as explained in Chapter 5. If it was not included in the charter, ask the team to estimate it now. Even if the rate was included in the charter, I recommend that you review it and confirm that the team still thinks it is a good estimate.

I know from experience that if you simply ask project team members to estimate the late penalty rate for their project, they will just stare at you with their mouths open. They will have no idea how to come up with the estimate. So don't ask that way. Instead, say something like, "Suppose the project dragged on for whatever reason for a month beyond the deadline. How much more would we spend on project overhead for an extra month, and how much would the opportunity cost be for an extra month?" You will probably need to identify and discuss the specific components of project overhead and the nature of the opportunity costs. The project customer should be involved in this discussion, since the customer probably knows the most about the opportunity cost. Eventually, the team will come up with some numbers, and when you add them up, they are usually astounded by how large the sum is. Then you divide the estimate for one month by 20 working days per month (assuming that weekends are not working days) to come up with a rate per working day. The estimate does not have to be accurate to within a few percentage points. We are just trying to get a ballpark understanding of how much a day is worth as we compress toward the project deadline.

Then you turn the question around to estimate the early payoff rate, which is the slope of the project-based cost line to the left of the deadline in Figure 10.1. Ask something like, "Now suppose we could finish the project a month ahead of the deadline. How much would we save in project overhead and opportunity cost?" Go through the same discussion process, add up the numbers and divide by 20 working days per month.

The late penalty rate should be greater than the early payoff rate. For the sake of an example, let's imagine that the late penalty rate is $3,000 per workday, and the early payoff rate is $1,000 per workday. These rates are much less than the rates we typically encounter on real projects, especially strategic projects.

Step 2: Identify Activities that Appear to Be Good Candidates to Compress on the First (or Next) Compression Step. Note that We Will Compress Only One Activity at a Time.

The activities that are the best candidates for compression tend to have several of the following characteristics.

First, activities that are candidates for compression *must be on the/a critical path*. There is no point in compressing non-critical activities. Compressing non-critical activities simply increases cost and stress and could damage quality without shortening the project duration.

If an activity is on a critical path *and* has one or more of the following characteristics, then it is usually an excellent candidate for compression.

- Activities in bottleneck positions in the project network; that is, all or most of the paths flow through the activity. Referring to the example network diagram in Figure 7.2, activities A and H are pure bottleneck activities, because they appear on all four paths through the network. Activities D and E each appear on two paths. Activities B, C, F, and G each appear on only one path. By compressing a bottleneck activity, you are compressing all the paths that flow through that activity. Now you see another advantage of having an explicit network diagram. It makes it easy to spot the bottleneck activities.
- Activities that take place early in the project. You cannot go back and compress an activity after you have performed it. Compress the early activities rather than betting on your ability to solve the problem by compressing activities later in the project. You may need to compress the later activities anyway if you fall behind schedule. So save the later activities as a risk management technique.
- Activities with relatively long normal durations. It is potentially easier to compress an activity whose normal duration is long (like 15 days) than an activity that is already short (like 3 days).
- Activities that can be compressed without compromising project quality or safety.
- Activities that use resources that are under the direct control of the project organization as contrasted with resources that are under the control of a vendor, contractor, external customer, government approval authority, or other outside source.
- Activities for which an easy and relatively inexpensive method exists to compress a significant amount of time out of the activity duration (e.g., express shipping).

If an activity is on a critical path *and* has one or more of the following characteristics, then it is often a good candidate for compression. But you should evaluate activities with these characteristics on a case-by-case basis. There are circumstances in which compressing these activities would be unwise.

- Activities that are labor intensive. Labor can be added in smaller increments and is generally a more manageable resource than other types of resources, such as equipment.
- Activities that require relatively low skill. The required resources are more plentiful and less expensive than relatively high skill resources. Also, such activities are usually less likely to compromise quality.
- Activities that are managed by a team member who delivers on commitments. However, you must be careful about burning out your best people! The old saying, "No good deed goes unpunished" tends to apply here. You really should be developing the less reliable individuals into more reliable team members.
- Activities that are subject to delay by common problems, such as inclement weather, equipment breakdowns, and so on. The risk management objective here is to reduce exposure to the common problems by getting the activity done quickly. "Make hay while the sun shines!"

Now we have a handful of activities on the current critical path(s) that look like good candidates for compression. For the sake of our example, let's imagine that we have identified two good candidates — activities J and M.

Step 3: Ask the Activity Manager of Each Candidate Activity Whether the Activity Can Be Compressed, and If So:

- How the activity could be compressed
- How much the activity duration would decrease
- How much the activity cost would increase.

In our example, the activity manager for activity J says that J could be compressed by paying a premium to the contractor to rush the work. The duration of J would decrease by 5 days, and the activity cost would increase by $7,500. The activity manager for activity M says that M could be compressed by working overtime. The duration of M would decrease by 4 days, and the activity cost would increase by $2,800.

Step 4: For Each Activity that Can Be Compressed (Based on the Results of Step 3), Determine If the Cost Trade-Off Is Attractive.

If the project completion date still exceeds the deadline, base the value of the time saved on the late penalty rate ($3,000 in our example). If the project has already been compressed to the deadline, base the value of time saved on the early payoff rate ($1,000 in our example).

So in our example, the cost trade-off for activity J would be attractive only if the project still exceeds the deadline. In that case, the 5 days saved would each be worth $3,000 or a total of $15,000, which is more than the $7,500 cost to compress the activity. But if the project is already within the deadline, the 5 days saved would only be worth $1,000 each or a total of $5,000, which is less than the cost of compressing the activity.

The trade-off for activity M, however, is attractive regardless of whether the project has already been compressed to the deadline. The value of 4 days saved is greater than the cost of compressing the activity no matter whether you base the value of the days saved on the late penalty rate or the early payoff rate.

Step 5: Select One (and Only One) Activity to Compress.

If one activity has a far more attractive cost trade-off than the other candidates, we usually select that activity to compress. If, however, several activities have almost equally attractive cost trade-offs, we consider other characteristics in making the selection, such as the characteristics listed in Step 2 above.

Step 6: Revise the Duration Estimate of the Activity Selected for Compression and Recalculate the Schedule.

Check to see how many days were actually saved on the project and whether the critical path(s) changed. If the critical path(s) changed and the number of days saved was less than the number expected so that the cost trade-off turned out to be unfavorable, go back to Step 5 and try a different activity to compress.

Step 7: Repeat Steps 2 through 6 Until No Further Compression Has a Favorable Cost Trade-Off; in Other Words, Until Further Compression Costs More in Added Activity-Based Cost Than It Saves in Project-Based Cost. You Have Found the Project Duration that Minimizes Total Project Cost.

If you have already compressed the project to the deadline or earlier, stop. If, however, the project still exceeds the deadline, you may be required to keep going (Steps 2 through 6) until you satisfy the deadline, even though total cost will begin to increase.

Compressing the Melbourne Plant Development Project

Now let's apply the compression process to the Melbourne Plant Development Project. As you know, the duration of the project based on the normal activity duration estimates is 96 working days, but the deadline is 70 working days. The initial critical path (see Figure 9.2) runs through the activities associated with the equipment. And as recorded in the project charter (see Figure 5.1), the late penalty rate is estimated as $8,000 per workday, and the early payoff rate is estimated as $6,000 per workday.

Compression Step 1

The first activity selected for compression is "Ocean Ship Equipment to Sydney." It is selected because its normal duration is 40 working days, which is over half the allowable duration of the project. It is doubtful that the project can be completed in 70 working days, if the duration of this activity remains at 40. The activity is compressed by leasing a large cargo aircraft to fly the equipment to Sydney, which will add $150,000 to the cost of the activity. The compressed duration is 10 working days, because the equipment still must pass through customs on departure from the United States and on arrival in Australia. In cases like this, it is not unusual for stakeholders to dismiss the idea without further analysis, because the added cost is "obviously too much to spend." We will analyze the cost trade-off in the next paragraph.

Figure 10.2 shows the impact of compressing the activity on the project schedule. Notice that the project duration has decreased from 96 to 73 working days and the critical path has shifted down to the activities associated with the building. Since we have not yet compressed to the deadline, all 23 of the days saved on the project duration are worth $8,000 per day. So the reduction in project-based cost is $184,000. Since the increase in activity-based cost is $150,000, the net saving on this step is $34,000. The results of this decision are recorded in the first row of the table shown in Figure 10.6 on page 141.

Compression Step 2

The activity selected for compression on the new critical path is "Develop Plant/Equipment Layout." This activity will be contracted out to a consultant, which will reduce the duration from 5 to 1 working day and will add $5,000 to the activity cost.

Figure 10.3 on page 136 shows the impact of this decision on the project schedule. The project duration has decreased to 70 working days, so we have already accomplished the objective

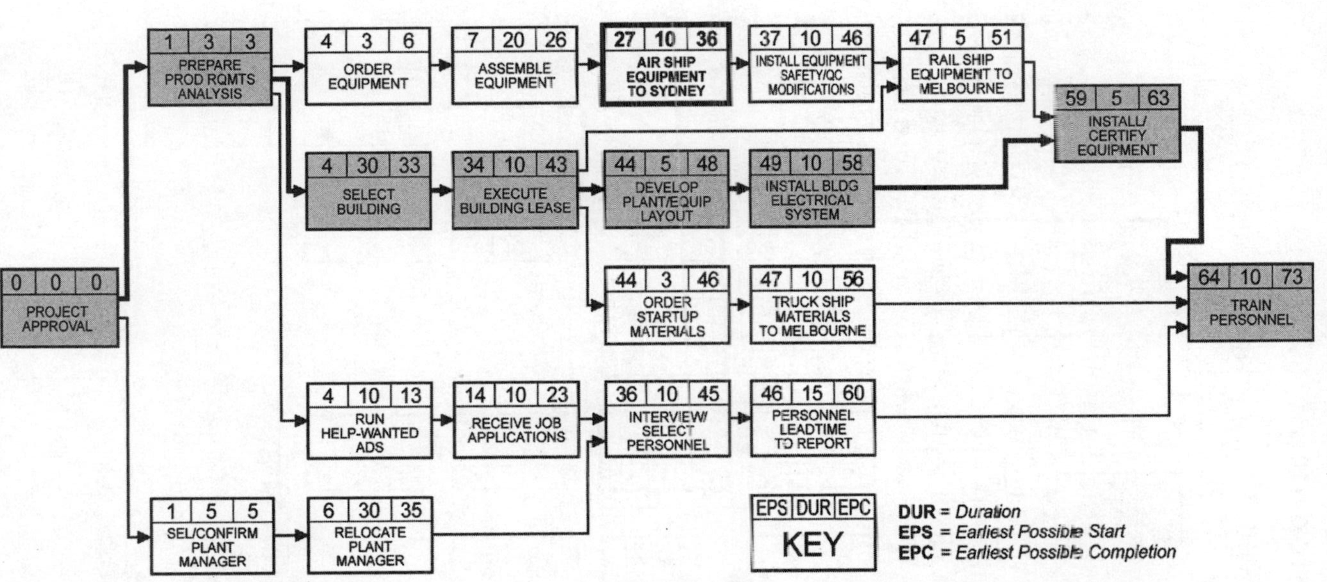

FIGURE 10.2 Compression Step 1 for Melbourne Plant Development Project

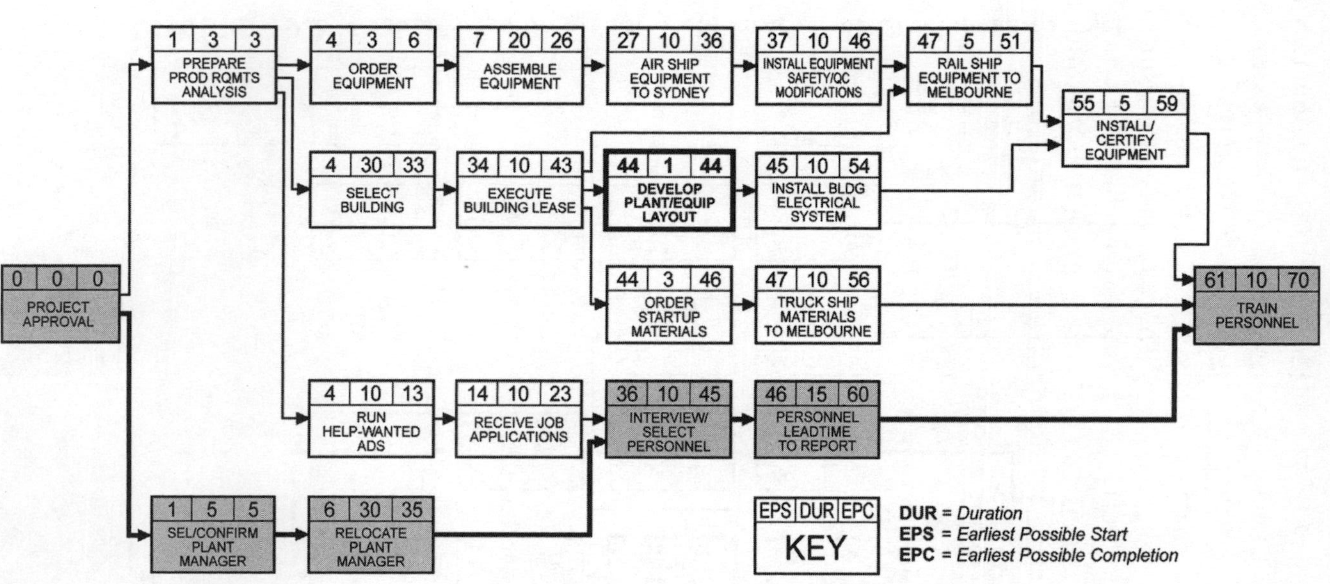

FIGURE 10.3 Compression Step 2 for Melbourne Plant Development Project

of compressing to the deadline by compressing only two activities! The critical path has shifted again down to the activities associated with the plant manager and operating personnel. The 3 days saved on the project duration are worth $24,000, and the cost of compressing the activity is $5,000, so the net saving on this step is $19,000. Again, the results are recorded in Figure 10.6. As would be expected in general, the net saving on each succeeding step tends to be less than the saving on the previous step as we approach the point of minimum total cost.

Compression Step 3

The next activity selected for compression is "Relocate Plant Manager." The plant manager will move temporarily into a furnished apartment to reduce the duration of the activity from 30 to 20 working days. This will add $1,000 to the cost of the activity.

Figure 10.4 shows the results of this decision. The project duration decreased to 69 working days, and the critical path shifted back up to the path associated with the building. The one day saved is worth only $6,000, since we have already compressed to the deadline. But since the added activity cost is only $1,000, the net saving is $5,000. The results are again tabulated in Figure 10.6. And as would be expected in general, the net saving is less than it was on the previous step.

Compression Step 4

The next activity selected for compression is "Install Building Electrical System." The electrical contractor will be paid a premium of $15,000 to compress the duration from 10 to 5 working days.

The results are shown in Figure 10.5 on page 139. The project duration decreased to 66 working days, so three more days were saved. The critical path split in two. The original critical path running through the equipment activities is critical again, so we finally got the full benefit of the 30 days that we

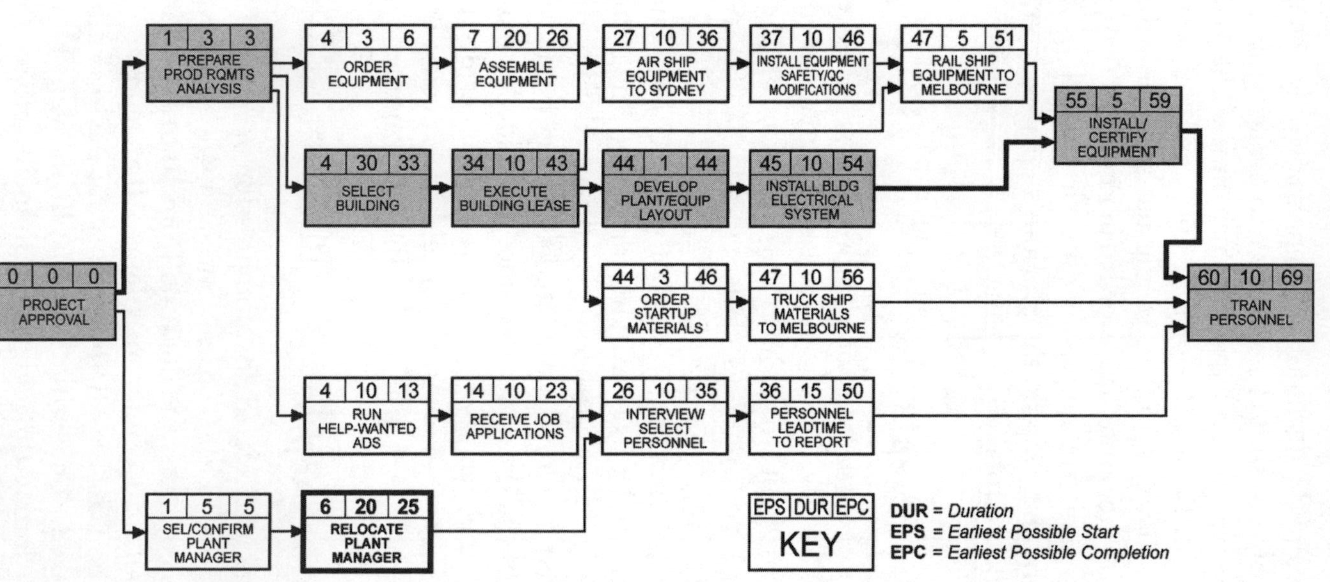

FIGURE 10.4 Compression Step 3 for Melbourne Plant Development Project

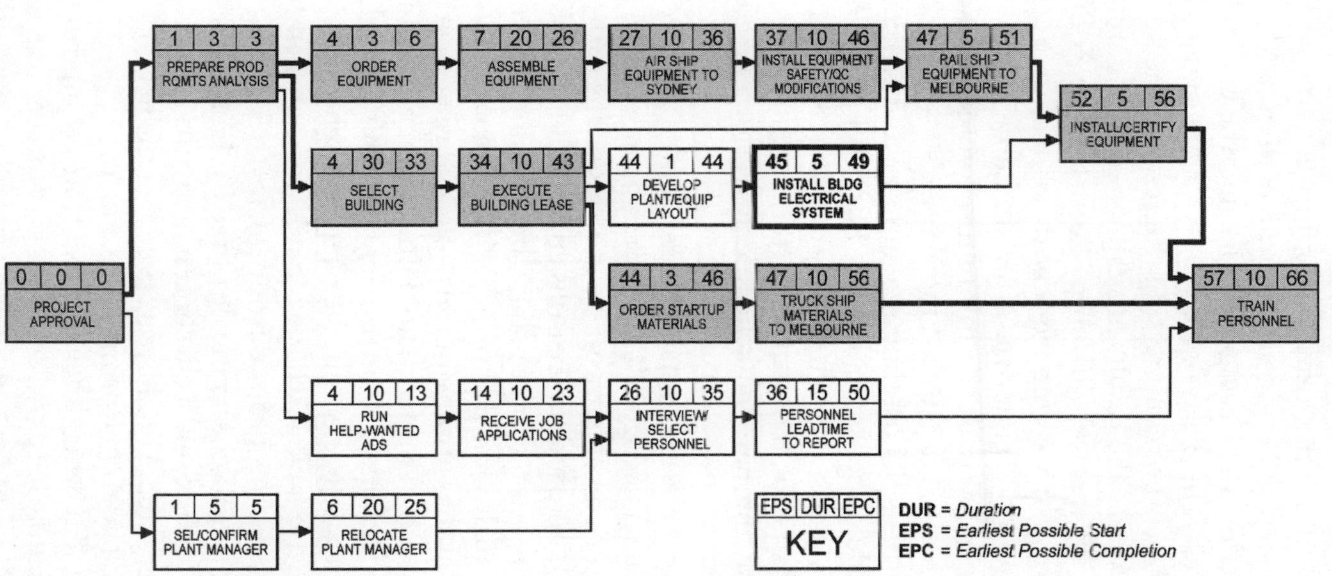

FIGURE 10.5 Compression Step 4 for Melbourne Plant Development Project

compressed out of the ocean shipping activity on the first compression step. The second critical path runs through the building selection and leasing activities and the materials acquisition activities. The 3 days saved are worth \$18,000, but after subtracting the cost of compressing the activity, the net saving is just \$3,000. Again, the results are tabulated in Figure 10.6.

This is where we will stop. Any further compression would require that we compress both critical paths, which is too expensive to be attractive. Now we know that the project duration associated with the minimum total project cost (the "?" in Figure 10.1) is 66 working days.

Figure 10.5 is the baseline schedule for the project; that is, the first schedule that is published. The EPS and EPC values shown in Figure 10.5 for each activity are the scheduled start and completion dates for the activity in the baseline schedule. We would publish the baseline schedule in various graphical and tabular formats.

You may be wondering why we never compressed the "Train Personnel" activity. This activity is in a pure bottleneck position, so compressing it would compress all the paths through the network. There are two reasons that we did not compress it. One reason is that compressing the training activity could compromise quality on this project. The second reason is that the activity is at the very end of the project. Rather than planning to compress it now, I prefer to hold onto the activity and think of it as an insurance policy. If the project falls behind schedule, I can always compress it to help me get back on schedule.

In summary, look at what we have accomplished here. We have compressed the project from 96 to 66 working days—a duration that actually beats the deadline by 4 days. We did it by compressing only four well-chosen activities, and we saved money on every step. Would you agree that the network diagram again was the key to performing this analysis?

To be candid, when I help project teams compress their real projects, we seldom keep track of the costs as precisely as illustrated in Figure 10.6. It just isn't necessary. On highly strategic projects,

Compression Step #	Activity Compressed & Method of Compression	Activity Duration		Project Duration	Added ABC	Savings in PBC	Net Savings
		BC	AC				
Start				96			
1	OCEAN SHIP EQUIPMENT TO SYDNEY Ship via leased cargo aircraft	40	10	73	$150,000	$184,000	$34,000
2	DEVELOP PLANT/ EQUIPMENT LAYOUT Contract out to a consultant	5	1	70	$5,000	$24,000	$19,000
3	RELOCATE PLANT MANGER Move temporarily into furnished apartment	30	20	69	$1,000	$6,000	$5,000
4	INSTALL BUILDING ELECTRICAL SYSTEM Pay contractor a premium to compress	10	5	66	$15,000	$18,000	$3,000

BC = Before Compressing ABC = Activity-Based Cost
AC = After Compressing PBC = Project-Based Cost

FIGURE 10.6 Steps and Results for Compressing Melbourne Plant Development Project

the opportunity costs are so huge (sometimes several hundred thousand dollars per day), that almost any action we can realistically take to compress critical activities is well worth doing. But we still compress only one activity at a time, and we always perform the schedule calculations after each step to determine the impact of our decision on the project duration and the critical path(s).

I have clients who have done amazing things with this compression concept and not just on individual projects. Some have used it to change their competitive strategy in ways that made their company far more successful. I challenge you to think about how this concept could be strategically advantageous to your business.

Advantages of Forward Scheduling and Strategic Compression

Early in Chapter 8, I said that project schedules developed using the back-scheduling or force-fitting approach almost never work. I discussed four problems associated with such schedules that cause the schedules to fail. As you can see, the forward scheduling and strategic compression approach overcomes all four of the problems associated with the back-scheduling approach.

1. You develop a specific plan for how each compressed activity will be performed within the shortened duration. You know that compressing the activity is feasible, and you recognize the added cost of compressing the activity.
2. Because the project team is devising methods to compress the activities and is involved in deciding which activities to compress, the team members maintain their commitment to the schedule and their sense of mutual accountability. The schedule is not "pie in the sky." Rather it is "our schedule for our project." There is a huge difference!

3. Only those activities that are on the critical path(s) and are good candidates for compression are being compressed. We are not wasting money and increasing stress by compressing activities that don't help shorten the project.
4. The schedule is based on starting and finishing each activity at the earliest possible time rather than the latest allowable time.

By using this approach you greatly improve the team's chances of completing the project by the deadline, while meeting quality/scope and cost expectations. Note again, that a network-based schedule is a prerequisite to using this approach. Again, this is by far *the easier way*!

For Advanced Discussion

A Word about Resource Planning and Budgeting

The remaining steps in the project planning process are resource planning and budgeting. Rather than devoting chapters to those topics, I have covered them in Appendices D and E for several reasons:

- Remember that the management of the time dimension of performance is the key to overall success on projects. Rather than getting bogged down in detailed discussions of resource planning and budgeting, I want to move on to the critically important project control process.
- Detailed resource planning and budgeting are not necessary on all projects. Detailed resource planning is most essential when resources are being shared across many projects of nearly equal priority. In such cases, resource planning must be

applied at the project portfolio level, rather than the individual project level. Highly strategic projects generally get whatever resources they need. Detailed budgeting is most essential when the project organization is being paid by an external customer to perform the project. Highly strategic projects are typically performed for internal customers, and most of the work is done by people who already work for the organization and are on salary.

- Some of my clients who would benefit from the application of detailed resource planning and/or budgeting simply cannot justify the effort and expense involved. The marginal benefit is not greater than the marginal cost.

Readers who need to know more about resource planning and/or project budgeting are invited to read Appendices D and/or E.

Key Takeaways

- Costs associated with projects fall into two general categories: (1) activity-based costs associated with the performance of the activities and (2) project-based costs associated with project overhead and opportunity cost.
- As the project is compressed from its initial "normal" duration, the project-based cost almost always decreases faster initially than the activity-based cost increases for the compressed activities. Therefore, the total project cost decreases until you reach a project duration that minimizes total cost.

- Involve the project team in devising methods to compress activities and deciding which activities to compress.
- To identify activities that are good candidates for compression, look for the characteristics presented in this chapter. Never compress an activity that is not on the/a critical path.
- Compress only one activity at a time, and use the schedule calculations to determine the impact of the compression on the activity duration and the critical path(s).

11

Monitor, Correct, and Update

Throughout this book we have emphasized the importance of project planning. But eventually (hopefully very quickly) we need to get beyond the planning process and begin executing the project. As with all complex human endeavors, projects rarely go exactly as planned. Let's look at how quickly things change at MeriwetherOutfitters.

Case Study: MeriwetherOutfitters

MeriwetherOutfitters.com is an Internet and mail-order retailer of outdoor recreation equipment and apparel. The company is currently developing a proprietary customer relationship management system to be called the

* This case is fictitious. Any similarity to actual, existing companies, individuals, or projects is purely coincidental.

(*continued*)

Scout System. Kelly Cunningham is the project manager reporting to project sponsor Cal Blevins, CIO. Alicia Pruitt, CEO, stops by Kelly's office.

"Hi, Alicia. To what do I owe the honor of your visit?" Kelly said.

"Oh, I was just meeting with Cal, and he was telling me about how hard you and your team have been working on the Scout System project. I just wanted to stop by and thank you guys for your great work. I believe this system is going to give us a major strategic advantage over our competition," Alicia said.

"Thank you, Alicia. I'll pass your comments on to the rest of the team. It will give them a real lift," Kelly replied as Alicia wandered over to a large, computer-generated project schedule pinned to the office wall. Alicia studied the chart for a moment.

"I see you're using project management software to support the planning and control of the project," she said.

"You bet! We would never undertake a project of this size and complexity without planning it thoroughly using the Project Pilot software."

"That's great," Alicia said, continuing to study the chart. "Let's see. Today is May 17, so according to this, you must be testing the customer buying history module."

"No. Don't pay any attention to that schedule," Kelly replied. "That's the schedule we developed last November. A lot has changed since then."

"Oh, I see. Well, as long as I'm here, could I take a look at the current schedule, just to get a feel for where the project stands?"

"I'm sorry, Alicia, but you're looking at the most current schedule I have. We have been so busy, we haven't had time to update it yet."

Questions

1. If you were Alicia Pruitt, what would you be thinking now?
2. How would you assess the chances that the Scout System will be delivered on time, within budget, and according to specifications?
3. What are the essential elements of an effective project control process?

In fact, Kelly, the project manager, doesn't really know where the project stands, and as a result, neither does the project sponsor or anyone else in the organization.

No battle plan survives contact with the enemy.

—Colin Powell

It's clear. A project control process is essential to (1) detect negative deviations from the plan, (2) solve problems, and (3) update the plan. Without a proactive control process, the project will get so far off the track that the plan loses its credibility. Once your project plan (especially the schedule) becomes nothing more than a decoration on the wall of the project manager's office, you've lost the ability to control the project.

Project control is largely a matter of discipline. It requires a no-nonsense approach to monitoring the status of the project and a firm determination to take corrective action as necessary. Project control involves a cyclical process that must not end until the project is completed. And the process must continually reinforce the team's commitment to the project plan and to each other as teammates. In my opinion, the ability to control projects effectively is the primary skill that separates world-class project managers from project manager want-to-bes.

By far the most effective approach to project control is for the project manager to hold face-to-face update meetings of the project team on a regular periodic basis. How often you hold the meetings depends on project size, complexity, and uncertainty, but we find that every two weeks is about right on most complex, strategic projects. When the team is geographically scattered so that face-to-face meetings are not practical, video-conferencing, teleconferencing, or Internet-based meetings (Sametime, WebEx, Live Meeting, etc.) are alternative approaches. However, two approaches that *don't work* are:

- For the project manager to communicate with the individual team members only one-on-one, or
- For the team to communicate exclusively electronically via e-mail or through a project web site.

The problem with these two approaches is that the team members never communicate directly with each other in a group context. The group interaction is essential for reinforcing the team's commitment to the project, as well as their sense of mutual accountability and support.

To make your project control meetings effective and efficient you, must structure them well and manage them skillfully. That means you want to focus the meetings mainly on the time (schedule and progress) dimension of project performance. Remember, the management of the time dimension is the key to success on all three dimensions of performance. Cost information can be gathered outside the context of the meetings. Quality-related information should arise naturally through the performance of activities specifically designed to ensure quality.

We suggest leading these meetings through four phases, which will be illustrated later in this chapter for the Melbourne Plant Development Project.

1. **Activity status reporting.** The project manager calls on the managers of current activities to report the status of their

activities. Has the activity been started, and if so, when? Has the activity been completed, and if so, when? If the activity has been started but has not been completed, when does the activity manager believe that it will be finished *or* what is the estimated remaining duration of the activity? What problems, if any, are being encountered on this activity? (Note that "percent complete" should *never* be used as a measure of activity progress. It is a largely meaningless measure of the past and says nothing about the future. Percent complete tends to cover up problems and undermine commitment to the project schedule. It is probably the most useless and potentially dangerous concept that has ever crept into the field of project management.)

2. **Determination of project status.** The activity status information is used in conjunction with the project network diagram to determine the status of the project as a whole. Project management software is helpful in making this determination quickly and accurately. Has the project fallen behind schedule? Has the critical path changed?
3. **Problem solving.** Solving problems is the main reason for having the meeting. The group works together in a mutually supportive manner to find ways to get the project back on track. How will we recover the days we've lost and get back on schedule? How will we handle the technical problem that has surfaced? Many alternatives may be suggested. With the project network diagram and the project management software tool, the team can perform what-if analyses to compare alternative solutions.
4. **Decision making, updating the schedule, and renewal of commitment.** In the final phase of the meeting, the team decides exactly what corrective actions to take. The schedule is updated to reflect the decisions made. Before the meeting adjourns, the project manager ensures that every member of the team understands the solution that has been chosen and is committed to fulfilling his or her specific responsibilities in implementing the solution.

Immediately following the meeting, the project manager produces a concise project status report, and distributes it to all project stakeholders, including the team members. The status report should do the following:

- Clearly state the current estimates of the project completion date and total project cost.
- Briefly describe any current problems or issues, as well as the actions being taken on each.
- Include as attachments the updated project schedule, typically in computer-generated tabular and graphical formats.

Then the project manager follows up with team members to ensure that they implement the agreed-upon corrective actions promptly and in a coordinated fashion. Meanwhile, team members continue to manage their activities on a day-to-day basis until it is time for the next meeting.

Controlling the Melbourne Plant Development Project

Now let's take a look at one control cycle for the Melbourne Plant Development Project. Project control meetings are held every two weeks. The first meeting was held after the first two weeks or 10 working days. Figure 11.1 simulates a computer-generated "Activity Update Input Form" that we use to collect the status information for the individual activities. The dates shown in the "Actual Start Date" and "Actual Finish Date" columns in Figure 11.1 were reported by the activity managers at the first control meeting. The dates shown in the "Scheduled Start Date" and "Scheduled Finish Date" columns were calculated by the project management software based on the activity status information provided by the activity managers. The form was generated following that first meeting and was the last item in the updated schedule package that was distributed with the

Melbourne Plant Development Project

Activity Update Input Form

Form generated at end of working day 10

Form used to update activity status at end of working day #: ______

Activity	Activity Manager	Planned Duration (Work Days)	Scheduled Start Date (Work Day #)	Actual Start Date (Work Day #)	Actual Finish Date (Work Day #)	Estimated Remaining Duration (Work Days)	Estimated Finish Date (Work Day #)	Scheduled Finish Date (Work Day #)	Critical ?
Prepare Production Requirements Analysis	Karlsson	3		1	3				
Select/Confirm Plant Manager	Baxter	5		1	4				
Order Equipment	Garcia	3		4	6				
Run Help-Wanted Ads	Puckett	10		4				13	
Select Building	Baxter	30		4				33	Critical
Relocate Plant Manager	MacBay	20		5				24	
Assemble Equipment	Garcia	20		7				26	Critical
Receive Job Applications	Puckett	10	14					23	
Interview/Select Personnel	MacBay	10	25					34	

FIGURE 11.1 Activity Update Input Form After First Control Meeting for Melbourne Plant Development Project

Activity	Activity Manager	Planned Duration (Work Days)	Scheduled Start Date (Work Day #)	Actual Start Date (Work Day #)	Actual Finish Date (Work Day #)	Estimated Remaining Duration (Work Days)	Estimated Finish Date (Work Day #)	Scheduled Finish Date (Work Day #)	Critical ?
Air Ship Equipment to Sydney	Garcia	10	27					36	Critical
Execute Building Lease	Chang	10	34					43	Critical
Personnel Leadtime to Report	Puckett	15	35					49	
Install Equipment Safety/QC Modifications	Schmidt	10	37					46	Critical
Develop Plant/ Equipment Layout	Karlsson	1	44					44	
Order Startup Materials	Garcia	3	44					46	Critical
Install Building Electrical System	Karlsson	5	45					49	
Rail Ship Equipment to Melbourne Plant	Schmidt	5	47					51	Critical
Truck Ship Materials to Melbourne Plant	Garcia	10	47					56	Critical
Install/Certify Equipment	Karlsson	5	52					56	Critical
Train Personnel	Moreno	10	57					66	Critical

FIGURE 11.1 *(Continued)*

status report from that meeting. The form will be used at the second meeting to collect the new activity status information. Please notice the following about Figure 11.1:

- On a real project, the values shown in all the start date and finish date columns would be calendar dates. Again, I am using working day numbers rather than calendar dates to make it easier for you to follow the scheduling calculations.
- The activities are sorted on the form in order of scheduled start date, so that as you work through the project, you move down the form. The activities could be sorted differently, such as by project deliverable or by team member, if you prefer.
- The first three activities have been started and completed. Since we now have the actual start and finish dates for those activities, the form no longer shows scheduled start and finish dates.
- The next four activities have been started but have not been completed. We no longer see the scheduled start dates, but the scheduled finish dates are still shown. You will see how we use the "Estimated Remaining Duration" and "Estimated Finish Date" columns for partially completed activities when we use the form to collect status information at the next meeting.
- So far, all the activities are running on or ahead of schedule. If you compare the start and finish dates shown on the form with the EPS and EPC values shown in the baseline schedule (Figure 10.5), you will see that they are the same, except that:
    - "Select/Confirm Plant Manager" was finished one day ahead of schedule (on day 4 rather than day 5), and therefore
    - The start and finish dates on the form for "Relocate Plant Manager," "Interview/Select Personnel," and "Personnel Leadtime to Report" are all one day ahead of the baseline schedule.

- Duncan MacBay was selected as the manager of the new plant, so he has joined the project team. He is now shown as the activity manager for "Relocate Plant Manager" and "Interview/Select Personnel" activities.

Now, we turn the clock forward two more weeks to the end of the fourth week (or 20th working day). Figure 11.2 shows how the Activity Update Input Form that was generated after the first meeting is used to collect the activity status information at the second meeting. The values shown in bold italics in Figure 11.2 were written on the form during the meeting based on status reports provided by the activity managers. These values were also entered into the project management software tool. Notice that:

- At the top of the form, we have recorded that we are updating the status of the activities at the end of working day 20.
- "Run Help-Wanted Ads" was completed on working day 13, right on schedule.
- "Select Building" is not yet finished. Due to problems in negotiating with a potential landlord, Baxter estimates that he needs until working day 36 to finish the activity, as shown in the "Estimated Finish Date" column. That means that he needs 16 more working days to finish the activity, as shown in the "Estimated Remaining Duration" column. Actually, "Estimated Remaining Duration" and "Estimated Finish Date" are two ways of asking the same question. I don't care which of these two questions the activity manager answers. Although Figure 11.2 shows the answers to both questions, we only need to record the answer given and enter it into the computer. The project management software immediately figures out the answer to the other question. Since the estimated finish date is 3 days later than the scheduled finish date, this activity is running behind schedule. And since this activity is critical (that is, it is on one or

Melbourne Plant Development Project

Activity Update Input Form

Form generated at end of working day 10

Form used to update activity status at end of working day #: 20

Activity	Activity Manager	Planned Duration (Work Days)	Scheduled Start Date (Work Day #)	Actual Start Date (Work Day #)	Actual Finish Date (Work Day #)	Estimated Remaining Duration (Work Days)	Estimated Finish Date (Work Day #)	Scheduled Finish Date (Work Day #)	Critical?
Prepare Production Requirements Analysis	Karlsson	3		1	3				
Select/Confirm Plant Manager	Baxter	5		1	4				
Order Equipment	Garcia	3		4	6				
Run Help-Wanted Ads	Puckett	10		4	*13*			13	
Select Building	Baxter	30		4		*16*	*36*	33	Critical
Relocate Plant Manager	MacBay	*20*		5		*2*	*22*	24	
Assemble Equipment	Garcia	20		7		*8*	*28*	26	Critical
Receive Job Applications	Puckett	10		*14*		*3*	*23*	23	
Interview/Select Personnel	MacBay	*20*	25					34	

FIGURE 11.2 Activity Update Input Form Showing Status Reports Collected at Second Control Meeting for Melbourne Plant Development Project

Activity	Activity Manager	Planned Duration (Work Days)	Scheduled Start Date (Work Day #)	Actual Start Date (Work Day #)	Actual Finish Date (Work Day #)	Estimated Remaining Duration (Work Days)	Estimated Finish Date (Work Day #)	Scheduled Finish Date (Work Day #)	Critical?
Air Ship Equipment to Sydney	Garcia	10	27					36	Critical
Execute Building Lease	Chang	10	34					43	Critical
Personnel Leadtime to Report	Puckett	15	35					49	
Install Equipment Safety/QC Modifications	Schmidt	10	37					46	Critical
Develop Plant/ Equipment Layout	Karlsson	1	44					44	
Order Startup Materials	Garcia	3	44					46	Critical
Install Building Electrical System	Karlsson	5	45					49	
Rail Ship Equipment to Melbourne Plant	Schmidt	5	47					51	Critical
Truck Ship Materials to Melbourne Plant	Garcia	10	47					56	Critical
Install/Certify Equipment	Karlsson	5	52					56	Critical
Train Personnel	Moreno	10	57					66	Critical

FIGURE 11.2 *(Continued)*

more critical paths), the scheduled completion date for the project will be delayed.

- "Relocate Plant Manager" is not finished, either. But MacBay has said that he will be on site and ready to report for work by the end of working day 22. That's an estimated remaining duration of 2 working days.
- The vendor for "Assemble Equipment" had a short labor strike since the last meeting. The vendor needs 8 more working days to complete the activity, which implies that the activity will be completed on working day 28. Again, we have a critical activity that is running behind schedule.
- "Run Help-Wanted Ads" actually started on working day 14, and it will be finished on working day 23, so that's 3 more working days for that activity.
- No other activities have started. In fact, no other activities are logically eligible to start. As a rule, I would never record an estimated remaining duration or an estimated finish date for an activity that has not actually started.
- Finally, Duncan MacBay has expressed disagreement with the 10-day estimated duration for "Interview/Select Personnel." Of course, he was not a member of the team when that duration was estimated. Since he is now the activity manager, we want him to be committed to the duration estimate. Based on the number of people to be hired and the number of good applications already received, MacBay estimates that he will need 20 working days to perform the activity.
- "Percent complete" was *not* used as a measure of progress on the activities. Instead, the activity managers for partially performed activities provided precise estimates and made personal commitments as to when their activities would be finished.

Clearly the project is running behind schedule, but it is not possible to know the exact situation without analyzing the combined impact of all the activity status information on the schedule. Fortunately, that is very easy to do, since we have a project network diagram and a project management software tool. Figure 11.3 shows the network diagram for what is left of the project. Notice that:

- Only activities that are not already finished are shown.
- The "Continue Project" node is like a "Start" node for the remaining activities, since we have more than one remaining activity that have no predecessors. There are finish-to-start precedence relationships from the "Continue Project" node to the first remaining activities. You don't have to create the "Continue Project" node or the precedence relationships; they are there conceptually and automatically, if necessary.
- The start date for what is left of the project (the EPS for the "Continue Project" node) is working day 20, since we are meeting at the end of day 20.
- The durations and EPC values for the four partially performed activities correspond to the estimated remaining durations and estimated finish dates shown for those activities in Figure 11.2.
- The forward pass calculations have been performed based on the status reports. The end date of the project has slipped from working day 66 to working day 69. We now have only one critical path, which runs through the building selection and leasing activities and the materials acquisition activities.

One common reaction to this situation is to do nothing to recover the 3 days that have been lost, because the scheduled finish date (working day 69) is still earlier than the project deadline (working day 70) as specified in the project charter. This reaction would be a huge mistake! If you have lost 3 days over the first 20 days of the project and you do nothing to recover those 3 days, how realistic is it to believe that you will finish the project by working day 69 or even by working day 70? You would have established the precedent of allowing "creeping schedule

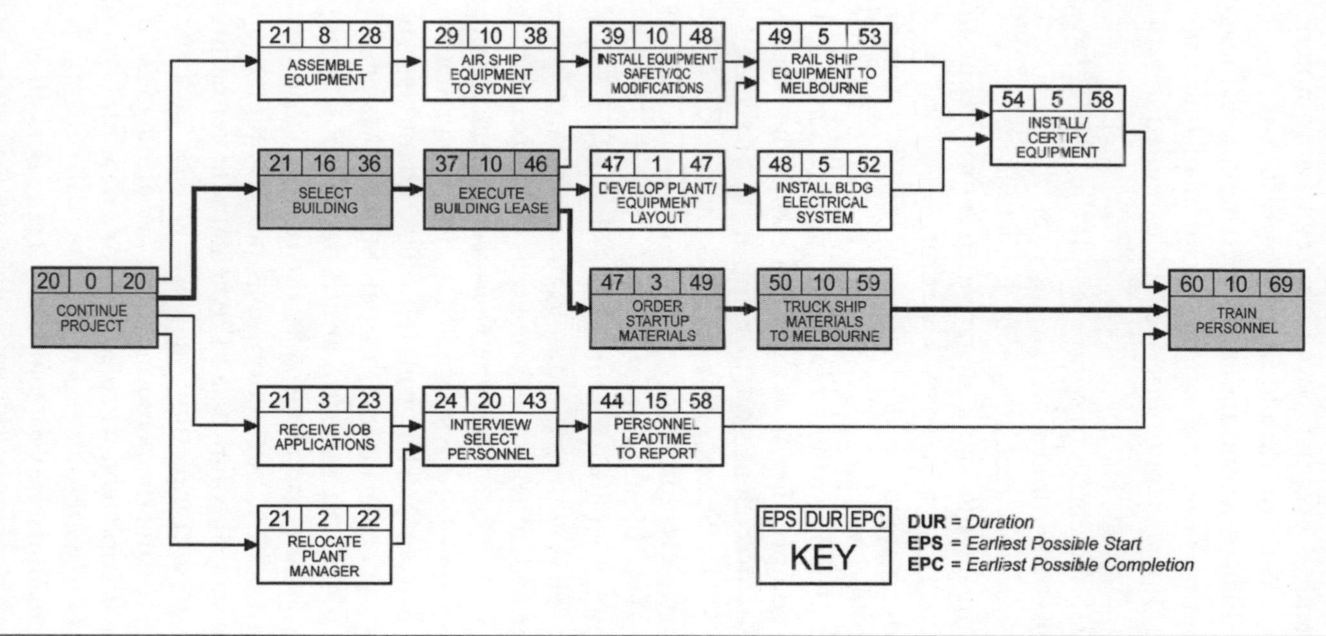

FIGURE 11.3 Melbourne Plant Development Project After 20 Working Days

slippage," and it will carry your project to a completion date much later than you would ever guess. Creeping schedule slippage is like compound interest in that the slippage does not just continue over the original scheduled duration of the project; the slippage continues over the extended duration. It is slippage on slippage!

The message here is to *be tenacious*. If the project has slipped by 3 working days, find a way to recover the 3 days. Put the project back on the track! Projects don't tend to correct themselves. Eliminate the small negative deviation from the plan before it becomes a very large deviation.

So the team members begin to suggest ways to compress the critical path by 3 working days. Soon a team member comes up with a great idea that will involve changing the network diagram rather than compressing an activity duration. The reason for the finish-to-start precedence relationship from "Execute Building Lease" to "Order Startup Materials" is that we do not want to order the materials until we can give the materials vendors a firm ship-to address. How about if we go ahead and order the materials immediately without giving a ship-to address and specify that the vendors should hold the orders until we contact them and provide the address? As far as the network diagram is concerned, we are disconnecting the successor end of the precedence arrow from "Order Startup Materials" and reconnecting it to "Truck Ship Materials to Melbourne Plant" as shown in Figure 11.4. We are taking "Order Startup Materials" completely out of the critical path, and it doesn't cost a dime!

Unfortunately, as indicated by the revised schedule calculations in Figure 11.4, this action does not completely solve the problem. In fact, it compressed the remainder of the project by only 1 day to a completion on working day 68, because the equipment path and the personnel path became critical. To solve the problem completely, we need to take 2 days off both of these two new critical paths.

So the team decides to compress "Train Personnel." It is an attractive candidate for compression, because it is the only activity

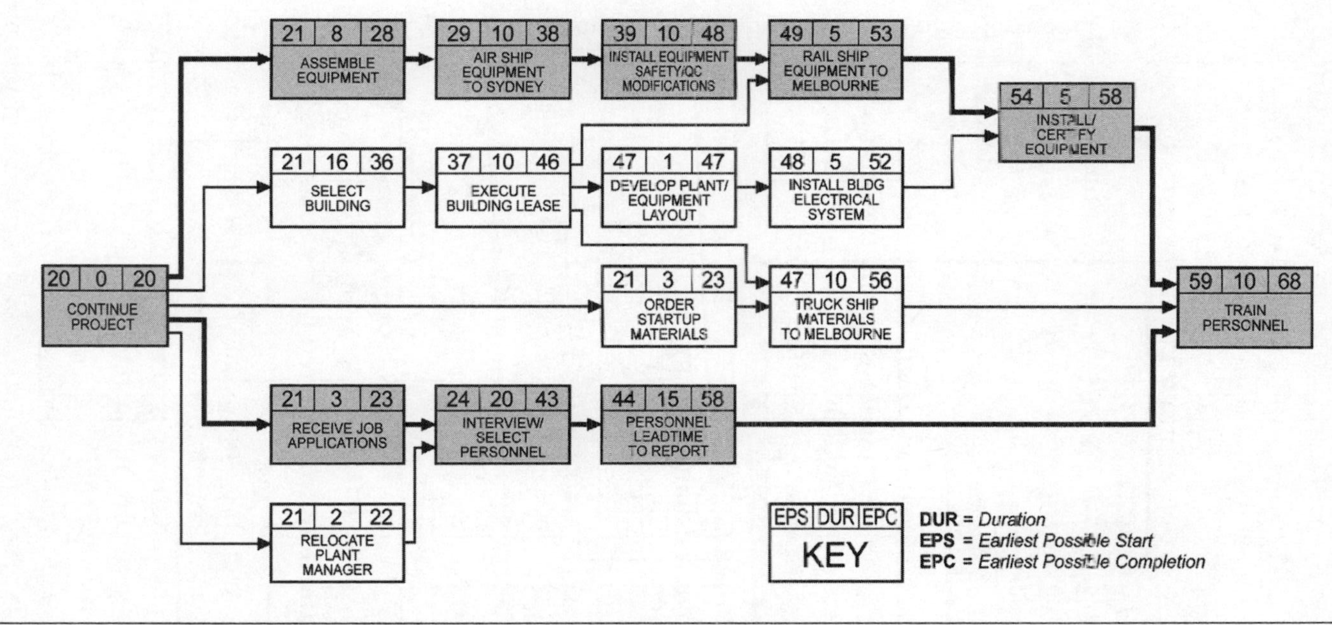

FIGURE 11.4 Schedule Calculations After Revision to Network Diagram

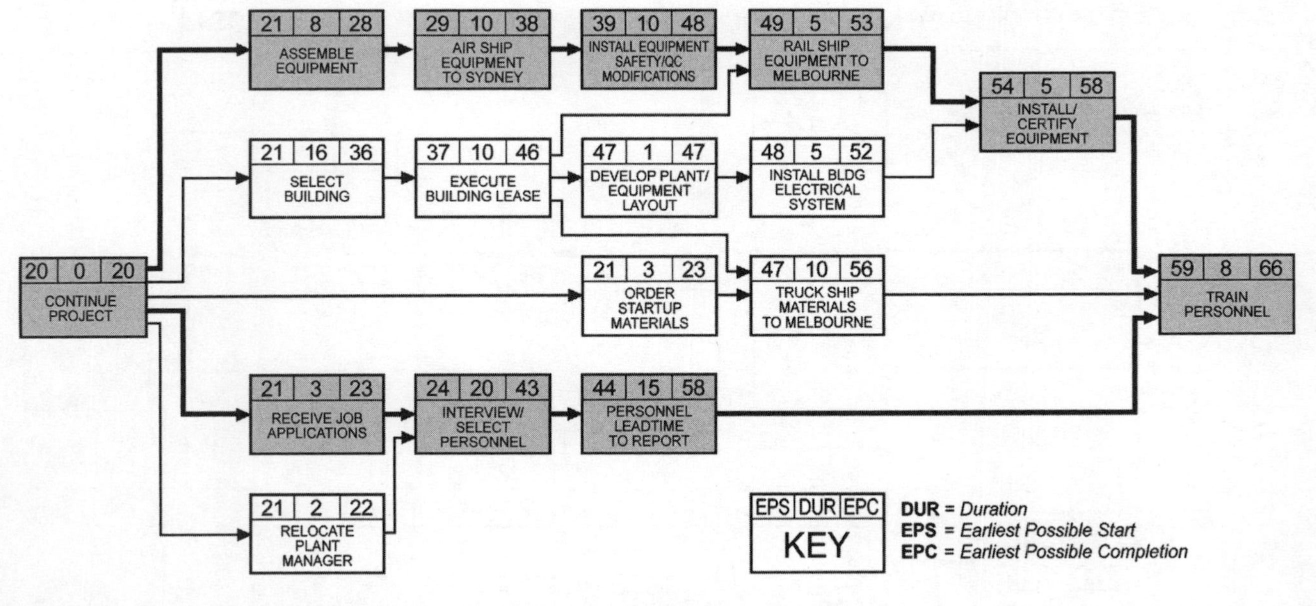

FIGURE 11.5 Updated Schedule After Compressing "Train Personnel"

that appears on both critical paths. It will be compressed to a duration of 8 working days by conducting 2 of the 10 days of training on Saturdays. So it is still a 10-day training program, which alleviates our concerns about potential quality issues. Since "Train Personnel" is in a pure bottleneck position in the network diagram, we have actually compressed every path through the project by 2 working days. The resulting schedule calculations are shown in Figure 11.5 on page 164. Problem solved! We are back to our baseline scheduled project completion date of working day 66. No creeping schedule slippage has been allowed. The updated schedule will be based on the EPS and EPC values shown in Figure 11.5.

Notice again how helpful the network diagram is in (1) determining the project status based on the activity status reports and (2) solving the problem of recovering the three lost days. In fact, without the diagram, we would be severely handicapped in attempting to control the project.

This disciplined and highly structured cyclical process is a powerful force in keeping projects on track and moving toward ultimate success. And it's *the easier way*!

Key Takeaways

- Without a proactive, disciplined, and highly structured approach to control, your project will probably fail, and your planning effort will have been wasted.
- The project control process must detect negative deviations from the plan, solve problems, and update the plan.
- Effective project control requires a current, credible schedule. If you allow the schedule to become outdated, you will have no basis for controlling the time dimension of your project.
- The most effective approach to project control involves periodic meetings of the project team. Approaches that avoid face-to-face communication among team members

are inferior in reinforcing mutual accountability, support, and commitment.

- Never use "percent complete" as a measure of progress on project activities. It is an undefined measure of the past. It tends to cover up problems, and it allows team members to avoid making a commitment about completing the activity.
- Be tenacious about solving problems and keeping the project on the track. Do not allow creeping schedule slippage.
- The network diagram is essential to determining the status of a complex project and to solving problems.
- Ensure that team members understand the corrective actions that have been decided upon and that they are committed to the implementation of those actions.

Build a System for Project Success

Companies that are adept at managing projects with a structured approach (ideally The Project Success Method) recognize the value of developing a project management system to facilitate that approach. A case in point is the architectural and engineering firm of Cohen and Phillips.

Case Study: Cohen and Phillips

Cohen and Phillips (C&P) is a successful architectural and engineering firm that specializes in commercial projects such as office buildings, shopping malls, hotels, and multiple-use complexes. Founded by Harvey Cohen and David Phillips, C&P employs approximately 100 architects and

* This case is fictitious. Any similarity to actual, existing companies, individuals, or projects is purely coincidental.

(*continued*)

engineers. At any given time, C&P is likely to be working on between 15 and 25 projects. Each project is managed by one of the more experienced architects or engineers. Individual staff members are shared across multiple projects as dictated by the need for their professional specializations. Harvey focuses on the marketing side of the business, and David manages service delivery operations.

It is late on the afternoon of December 31st, and everyone except Harvey and David has left the office to celebrate New Year's Eve. Harvey and David are relaxing in Harvey's office, reflecting on the year just completed.

"Well, David, it's been another record year for C&P. I guess we must be doing something right," Harvey said.

"I'd say we're doing a lot of things right. Your rain-making ability is fantastic—actually almost scary. We have terrific people and a client base that lots of A&E firms would kill for. I must admit, though, that I'm starting to worry about our ability to manage our service delivery operations in the future, if we continue to grow at this rate."

"What specifically are you concerned about, David?"

"Several things. First, more than half of our most experienced project managers will retire within the next five years."

"Okay, but we have some good junior people," Harvey said. "Don't you think that some of them will be able to fill the void?"

"They should be able to, but we have no process to make that happen. We've always been fortunate that some of our people seemed to be able to manage projects reasonably well. We've never had a formal program for developing our project managers." David added.

"Which leads me to my next concern," he continued. "Even now, the approaches used by our project managers are not at all consistent. We have no standard methodology. They use different planning and control processes, different software tools, and different formats for planning documents and reports."

"Is consistency really all that important, as long as the project managers are producing good results?"

"Yes, consistency is important," David replied. "How can we develop effective new project managers if we haven't adopted a structured and consistent approach to managing our projects? Plus, the inconsistency creates confusion for our people—most of whom are working on several projects under different project managers at any given time."

"I see your point," Harvey said. "So, we need a consistent project management methodology and a program for developing new project managers. What else are you concerned about?"

"We're having continuing problems managing the workload for our people, and the problem seems to be getting more severe and complex. It's starting to have a negative impact on both our project performance and our staff morale," David said.

"For example, Roberta Collins has been working 60 hours a week for the last month because activities that require her expertise in lighting systems design have all come up at the same time on three different projects. In addition to the fact that Roberta is working to the point of exhaustion, all three of those projects have begun to fall behind schedule, because she can't keep up," he explained.

"We're doing so well, I would have no objection to hiring another specialist in lighting systems design, if that's what we need," Harvey said.

"But it's not clear that we really need another permanent person—at least not yet. Just two months ago, Roberta didn't have enough work to keep her busy, and Gerhard Mueller was the one who was overworked on HVAC systems design activities.

"What we need is the ability to anticipate these shifting work overloads and take steps in advance to minimize or alleviate them. As it is now, we don't even realize we have the problem until we are already suffering from its effects. By then, our options for dealing with the overload are pretty limited."

Questions

The concerns that David is describing can be addressed through the design and implementation of a project management system for his organization.

1. What could be some of the components of a project management system?
2. What factors would affect the design of project management systems for different organizations?
3. How might you create the capability to anticipate work overloads in a situation where people are shared across multiple projects?

C&P needs a project management system if it is going to continue to successfully manage a growing number of projects. **A project management system is an integrated set of organizational and technological elements that supports the effective application of project management processes on your projects.**

In other words, the project management system should make it easier and more efficient to use The Project Success Method. The system is not specific to a single project, but is a permanent infrastructure that is intended for use on a continuing stream of projects. Some of the typical elements of a project management system are the following:

- Standard processes for defining, planning, and controlling projects (ideally the processes of The Project Success Method).

- Project management policies and procedures manual.
- Project management software tool and other related software.
- Standard formats for planning documents and control reports.
- Standard codes for identifying cost categories, resource types, etc.
- Group communications technologies, such as videoconferencing, for use by project teams.
- Template planning documents (charters, work breakdown structures, project network diagrams, schedules, budgets) for common types of projects.

Some organizations create a "project management office" or "PMO," which is a staff function that has responsibility for developing and maintaining the project management system. The PMO would also perform all project portfolio-level analyses. For example, in the Cohen and Phillips case, the PMO would be responsible for rolling up projected workloads for each resource (e.g., each person) across all projects in order to anticipate resource overloads. (See Appendix D for an explanation of how this can be done.) The PMO also trains, coaches, and assists project managers in the application of the project management methodology and the project management system. The PMO should ensure that the effective practice of project management continues and improves over the long term, as individuals join and leave the organization. (See Appendix G for more detail on the PMO.)

Just as you would outfit a mountain climbing team differently depending on the type of mountain it intended to climb and the conditions under which it will do it, project management systems must be tailored to the environment in which they will operate. In creating a project management system, some key questions are:

- How many projects do you usually have going on at any given time?

- Are your project customers internal or external to your organization—or both?
- Is your organization structured around functions or projects, or is it a matrix structure?
- How large are your projects in terms of duration, cost, number of people/organizations involved, and number of activities?
- How complex are your projects, and how much uncertainty is involved?
- How tightly constrained are your project durations, budgets, and the resources available to work on your projects?
- Are resources shared across multiple projects?
- How skilled are your project managers in terms of the project management methodology, leadership ability, and the use of software tools?

You must take into consideration all of these factors, among others, when developing an effective project management system for an organization. A well-designed project management system will make it much easier to apply The Project Success Method and to achieve project success. And thanks to human nature, we are all much more likely to use an approach that is easy as well as effective.

Key Takeaways

- Design and build a system consisting of an integrated set of organizational and technical elements to support the ongoing effective application of The Project Success Method on your organization's projects.
- Ensure that some person or group in your organization has ongoing responsibility for building, maintaining, and improving your project management system.
- In designing your project management system, consider the characteristics of your business, your organization, your projects, and your people.

13

Overcome the Objections

As reasonable and rational as The Project Success Method is, we have found that it is often met with objections from the people who will be affected. On the spur of the moment, they may be able to come up with a host of objections, as they did at New Millennium Manufacturing Company, the firm implementing an enterprise management information system. (This company was previously mentioned in Chapters 5 and 6.)

Case Study: New Millennium Manufacturing Co.

Les McDonald (Chief Information Officer) is wrapping up the monthly meeting with all the project managers in the Information Systems and Technology Department.

* This case is fictitious. Any similarity to actual, existing companies, individuals, or projects is purely coincidental.

(*continued*)

"Before we adjourn, let me mention something that has been on my mind for some time now," Les said. "I would like to let you know what I've been thinking about and get your feedback. As you know, virtually everything we do in the IST Department is a project. It seems to me that we've struggled with how to manage our projects, and it has been taking a toll on us in both our project performance and the quality of our work lives. I'd like for us to implement a more structured and consistent approach to project management," he continued.

"I've identified a consulting firm that specializes in project management. They can provide us with training in a proven and practical approach to managing projects. They can also provide consulting assistance to our project teams as we begin to use the approach. Ultimately, they can help us implement a project management system that is tailored to our situation and needs," he added.

"Les, that project management stuff takes a lot of time," Beth Robertson quickly replied. "I don't have enough time now to get all my work done. The last thing I need is something else that will demand more time that I just don't have."

Then Raoul Ibrahim spoke up, "I attended a project management seminar several years ago. I got the impression that the techniques they were teaching would work fine for construction projects, where there is relatively little uncertainty, but that they wouldn't be very useful on our projects."

"Les, wouldn't this cost a lot of money?" added Tasha Sadoski. "I thought we were supposed to be pinching every penny this year."

"I don't even understand why you are considering this, Les," Alex St. John said. "I thought we were doing pretty well on our projects. I say, 'If it ain't broke, don't fix it!' "

Questions

1. Other than the specific concerns that are being expressed by the project managers, what may be motivating their objections to the implementation of a structured and consistent approach to project management?
2. Can you think of other concerns or objections that might be raised?
3. How would you respond to each of the concerns/ objections?

Les may have been surprised to encounter immediate objections from every corner. But our experience has shown that this is a typical reaction. People tend to resist change, when they view it as threatening. Their objections often are a smoke screen to hide their fear, rather than genuine concerns. The actual motivations behind these concerns may even be subconscious and unclear to the individuals voicing the concerns.

There are several reasons why the adoption of structured project management may appear threatening to the people affected. For one thing, it imposes clear responsibilities, discipline, and accountability on project team members. Shifting the "worry curve" (as explained in Chapter 3) can also be an uncomfortable prospect at first. Adoption of structured project management can also seem threatening, because it requires the mastery of new skills, which can be a frightening challenge for some people.

The key point for managers is that responding to the specific concerns expressed by their people may not be sufficient to deal effectively with the underlying, driving force of resistance. People must be reassured that The Project Success Method will not be used as a whip to coerce or punish them. You must convince them that the change is intended to improve the quality of their work life as well as to improve project performance.

Still, it is necessary to respond to the stated objections. Below are the most common objections and our response to each.

1. It is too time consuming.

   This is the most common and usually the first objection you will hear. People point out that the processes of defining, planning, and controlling projects consume time that they do not have to spare. They can't get all their work done now, so the imposition of structured project management processes will only make the situation worse. We have two responses to this concern.

   a. As people gain experience in the application of The Project Success Method, they are able to perform those processes faster and more efficiently. The required skills become more automatic, as people actually develop new ways of thinking about projects. The software tools, template plans, and standard formats for documents/reports also speed up the process. Most people will accept this first response as true.
   b. Team members generally must take on faith the second and more important response until they see it demonstrated to be true. The time invested in the processes of defining, planning, and controlling projects will be more than repaid in the time saved that would otherwise have been wasted fighting the fires and untangling the foul-ups that are prevented by using The Project Success Method. In other words, although The Project Success Method clearly does involve an investment of time, the ultimate result is a net saving of time.

2. It won't work on our projects.

   People will proclaim that structured project management processes are well suited to projects performed by other organizations, but not to the projects that they are required to perform. They claim that their projects are unique. Their projects are so ill-defined, so complex, involve so much uncertainty (and so on) that it is impossible to plan and estimate them. Again, we offer two responses.

   a. We are always tempted to ask people who voice this objection to show us the approach they use to manage their projects, which is more effective than The Project Success Method. We admit this response is somewhat flippant, but we have yet to be shown such an approach. The answer is always some version of "muddling through."
   b. The second response to this objection is dead serious, and people know that it is true even if they aren't willing to admit it. The more ill-defined, complex, uncertain, (etc.) your projects are, the more you need to apply structured processes to define, plan, and control them. In other words, the harder it is to use The Project Success Method, the more important it is to do exactly that. Of course, people ultimately discover that their projects are not really that much different from the projects performed by other organizations.

3. It will cost too much.

   Adopting The Project Success Method will typically involve initial costs for training, software, and perhaps consulting assistance. Ongoing costs may include the salaries of people who staff a project management office. But these costs typically pale in comparison to the cost of just one blown project that is of strategic importance to the organization. The cost of implementing and applying The Project Success Method is the premium you pay for a very inexpensive insurance policy to protect yourself and your organization against project failures. The payback period on an investment in effective project management is extremely short.

4. It is too complicated.

   This is simply untrue. Actually, The Project Success Method involves the application of straightforward logic and simple arithmetic. And of course, your project management software tool will do the calculations for you. We cannot deny that practitioners must master the required concepts, principles, and analytical skills. Our experience proves that we can impart this knowledge in only two days of intensive training. Another day of training may be required to master the user skills for the software tool to be employed. Thus, in a mere three days of training, most people are ready to participate in or even lead the structured processes of The Project Success Method for defining, planning, and controlling projects. How complicated can it be? After all, it is the easier way!

5. It is too inflexible.

   This concern may be expressed about The Project Success Method itself or about the project plans that result from its application.

   a. To the extent that people view The Project Success Method as inflexible, we would argue that if the opposite of inflexibility is inconsistency, then inflexibility is a good thing. We have seen too many cases in which people have succumbed to the temptation to stray from the structured processes that we advocate only to discover that they have created real problems for themselves. When you know the path that always leads to the desired destination, taking an uncharted shortcut can be a dangerous gamble.
   b. Some people believe that The Project Success Method leads to inflexible project plans. Such people often regard any reasonably detailed plan as inflexible. Or they may have previously used planning processes that really are inflexible, such as the development of project schedules that are not network-based (as explained in Chapter 7). Actually, one of the real strengths of the structured processes we advocate for defining, planning, and controlling projects is that they require the development of a

fairly detailed plan, but then *allow for and facilitate adjustments to the plan*, as circumstances change and new information becomes available.

6. We don't need it. We're doing OK without it.
   a. People who voice this objection usually have an unrealistic view of how well their organization executes projects. They quickly discount the dropped elements of project scope, the compromised quality, the missed deadlines, and the budget overruns that characterize their projects. They overlook the crises, stress, and conflict, or they view such dynamics as natural and inevitable in projects. Worse yet, some people actually seem to thrive—at least in the short run—on turmoil and heroic efforts. Such people don't recognize that their project management processes are broken, and they must be shown the evidence.
   b. Even an organization that has not experienced significant project failure should recognize the opportunity, value, and necessity of improving its project management capability as a strategic core competency. In this world of ever-escalating global competition, any organization that is not continuously improving its critical skills will soon be overtaken by a competitor who is.

Key Takeaways

- Expect people in your organization to resist the implementation of any structured project management processes, including The Project Success Method.
- Be prepared with responses to the most typically expressed objections/concerns.
- Recognize that the driving force behind the stated objections may be an unstated and perhaps subconscious feeling of being threatened by the imposition of clear responsibilities, discipline, and accountability as well as by the requirement to learn new skills.

14

Apply the Power of Project Success

The benefits that you and your organization receive from the skilled and disciplined application of The Project Success Method go far beyond your expectations. These benefits of project success fall into three categories.

1. **The benefits to the projects themselves.** Projects are more successful than ever before. They are completed in accordance with quality specifications, on schedule, and within budget. Project stakeholders are satisfied, if not absolutely delighted!
2. **The benefits to the people who work on projects.** Project teams take ownership of their projects and commit to their project plans. Their roles and responsibilities in the project are clarified. They feel the motivating power of mutual accountability and support among their teammates. Communication is improved. Problems are prevented, or at

least detected earlier and solved more easily. Frustration, stress, and conflict are minimized. The quality of their work life is dramatically improved!

3. **The benefits to the competitiveness of the company.** The ability to execute all sorts of projects faster, with higher quality, and at lower cost than your competition is a major source of competitive advantage. Because of its increased confidence in the organization's ability to execute projects, senior management is more willing to undertake strategic initiatives. Change actually happens, and vision is transformed into reality!

Learn and apply The Project Success Method, and expect to enjoy all three types of benefits to your organization. And in doing so, you are developing and applying skills that will enhance your own professional career. People who have demonstrated the consistent ability to manage complex projects successfully are extremely rare and highly valued in today's business world. They are the few who have mastered the easier way!

Key Takeaways

The organizational benefits of The Project Success Method fall into three categories:

- Successful performance of individual projects.
- Quality of work life improvements for project team members.
- Competitive advantage to the company that can consistently execute strategic projects successfully.

In addition to the benefits that accrue to the organization is the personal career advantage that accrues to individuals who have mastered The Project Success Method.

APPENDICES

APPENDIX A

Developing Operating Procedures for Projects Involving Multiple Organizations Using a Linear Responsibility Chart

One of the challenges of managing projects that involve several (perhaps many) organizations is that the group has no pre-established procedures for handling actions that cross organizational boundaries. Such actions often include the following:

- Technical decisions (e.g., specification or design changes)
- Managerial decisions (e.g., schedule changes)
- Administrative processes (e.g., issuing payments)
- Project activities that involve more than one organization (e.g., approvals or inspections, placing purchase orders)

If such inter-organizational actions are not anticipated and procedures put in place to guide their performance, confusion and miscommunication will result, which will lead to unnecessary delays, wasted resources, and potentially even conflict among the organizations.

The development of operating procedures for multi-organizational projects can be facilitated by the use of a tool known as a "liner responsibility chart" (LRC). Consider the hypothetical and simplified example illustrated in Figure A.1. Cavendish Chemicals is planning the design and construction of its new Plant Clearwater. The project will involve the individuals, departments, and organizations shown in the columns of the chart. The inter-organizational actions that can be anticipated on this project are listed in the rows of the chart. Several responsibility codes (letters) are defined in the upper left corner, and these codes are used in each cell of the chart to indicate the responsibility(s) of the entity in that column relative to the action in that row. By reading the codes in any row of the LRC, it is possible to ascertain an overview of the procedure for the action associated with that row.

The LRC is not intended to be an end in itself. Rather, the LRC is an efficient tool that is used to collect and verify information about how the organizations intend to work together, so that written procedures for each action can be developed quickly and with minimum rework. The process involves several steps as follows:

1. Identify the individuals, departments, and organizations that should be represented in the chart and develop the column headings for those entities.
2. Develop an initial set of responsibility codes, such as the codes shown in the example.
3. Interview the project manager. Make an audio recording of the interview. Ask the project manager to:
   a. Identify inter-organizational actions that should be included in the chart and ultimately in the project procedures manual. Enter these actions in the rows of the chart.
   b. Talk through the procedure for each action as he or she would prefer that it be performed. Enter responsibility codes into the cells of the chart to capture the procedure as described. If necessary, create additional responsibility codes.

Cavendish Chemicals, Inc.

Linear Responsibility Chart for Design and Construction of Plant Clearwater

RESPONSIBILITY CODES

- **A** Requests/Initiates
- **B** Performs/Takes Action
- **C** Must Be Consulted
- **D** Must Approve
- **E** Must Be Informed

	INDIVIDUAL/ORGANIZATION									
	Cavendish Chemicals									
ACTION	**VP-Production**	**Project Manager**	**Process Engineering**	**Plant Engineering**	**Architect**	**General Contractor**	**Subcontractors**	**Equipment Vendors**	**EPA**	**County Bldg. Inspector**
Process design specification changes	D	E	A/B	C	E	E		E	D	
Plant design changes	E	E	C	A/B	C	C	E		E	D
Design schedule changes	D	B	A/C	A/C		C				
Construction schedule changes	D	B		A	C	C	E	E		
County inspections		E		E	E	A	E			B/D
EPA inspections		A	E	E					B/D	
Owner inspections	E	B/D			E	E				
Payments	B	D			D	A	A	A		

FIGURE A.1 Example Linear Responsibility Chart

4. Interview other key individuals who are identified in the LRC or who represent departments or organizations identified in the chart. The order in which these interviews are conducted is not critical. Again, make an audio recording of each interview. Show each interviewee the actions that have been entered into the LRC by previous interviewees. Ask the interviewee to identify additional actions that should be included and to describe the preferred procedure. Again, enter the appropriate codes in the LRC, and create additional responsibility codes if necessary.
5. When the interviews have been completed, hold a meeting of the key individuals who are identified in the LRC or who represent departments or organizations identified in the LRC. Make an audio recording of the meeting. Give out copies of the LRC.
   a. Explain the procedure for each action as described by the responsibility codes. Ask for comments, suggestions, or concerns on the procedure for each action. Seek consensus on all changes. Make changes to the codes as appropriate.
   b. Ask for any additional actions that should be added to the LRC. Have the group discuss the preferred procedure for any such actions and record the appropriate codes on the LRC. Again, seek consensus.
6. Using the LRC (and audio recordings as necessary), develop a project procedures manual. Each row on the LRC should be converted to a written procedure. Each procedure should have:
   a. Date and draft number
   b. Action name/description (e.g., "Construction schedule changes")
   c. Statement of the procedure based on the codes in the LRC. In addition, the statement may contain details, such as:
      (1) When making a submittal, exactly what documentation to provide and to whom it should be sent.

(2) How long an entity normally has to review and act on an item submitted for its approval or other action.

(3) Who should receive copies of certain communications.

(4) Whether hard copy or electronic communication are required/allowed.

d. Signature lines for the project manager and for other key individuals who are identified in the LRC or who represent departments or organizations identified in the LRC. The signatures indicate that these key individuals approve the procedure and that they will follow and require other members of their organization to follow the procedure.

In addition to the individual procedures, the procedures manual should contain:

(1) A table of contents

(2) A directory of key individuals involved in the project, including phone numbers, mailing addresses, and email addresses

(3) The final LRC on which the procedures are based

(4) A glossary of terms, if necessary

7. Distribute the procedures manual to all involved organizations in hard copy and/or electronic format.

The early development of a procedures manual as described above has proven invaluable on projects involving multiple organizations. The application of the LRC in the context of the steps outlined above greatly facilitates the process, and it ensures that the procedures manual is complete and represents consensus among the involved organizations.

APPENDIX B

Generalized Precedence Diagramming

In Chapter 7, I explained how to develop project network diagrams using the simplest type of precedence relationship—that is, a finish-to-start ("FS") relationship, with no duration associated with the precedence relationships. I also mentioned that other more complex types of precedence relationships are supported by the popular project management software tools. But I recommended that you use only the simplest type of precedence relationship to the extent possible, even if you have to break your activities into a little more detail to capture the intended logic. Although it is not always possible to capture the intended logic using only the simplest type of relationship, it usually is possible, and there are two reasons for doing so whenever possible:

- The logic of your network diagram will be much easier to understand.
- The results of the scheduling calculations made by your project management software tool will be much easier to interpret.

In this appendix, I will explain the additional complexities associated with "Generalized Precedence Diagramming." For the most commonly used types of complex precedence relationships, I will show you how to capture the same logic using the simple FS relationships with no associated duration.

Generalized Precedence Diagramming introduces either or both of two additional types of complexity into a precedence relationship:

- A duration is associated with the precedence relationship. The duration can be a positive number (of workdays, for example), in which case it is called a "lag," or it can be a negative number, in which case it is called an "overlap."
- The driving logic between the predecessor activity and the successor activity is something other than finish-to-start. The other types of driving logic, in order of frequency of use on real projects, are:
  - Start-to-start (SS): The start of the predecessor drives the start of the successor.
  - Finish-to-finish (FF): The finish of the predecessor drives the finish of the successor.
  - Start-to-finish (SF): The start of the predecessor drives the finish of the successor.

Now let's look at the three most common types of complex precedence relationships, so that you understand what they mean, but more important, so that you know how to capture the same logic using only FS relationships with no lags. In each case, I will illustrate the relationship with an example from a real project.

Finish-to-Start with a Lag. A facility development project involved ordering some equipment, shipping the equipment from the vendor to the facility, and installing the equipment. You could capture the logic as shown in Figure B.1a. Notice that

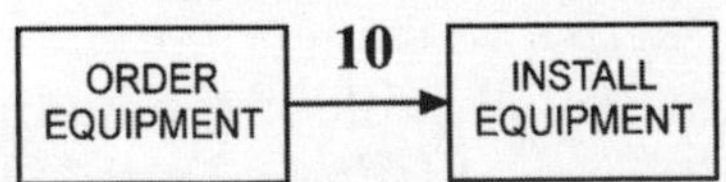

FIGURE B.1a **Finish-to-Start with Lag**

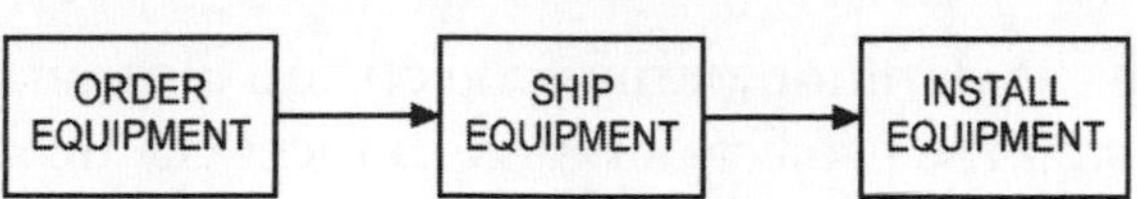

FIGURE B.1b Lag Replaced by Activity

there is no activity node for the shipping of the equipment. Instead, the time required to ship the equipment is captured in the lag of 10 days between the ordering activity and the installation activity. Some people would draw the diagram this way, because the shipping is one of those special case activities that involve waiting, rather than doing, from the project team's point of view. I would *never* treat the shipping as a lag. Instead, I would treat it as an activity as shown in Figure B.1b. Why? For two very important reasons:

1. I want a member of the project team to take responsibility for tracking the shipment. We routinely appoint a team member to manage each activity, but I have never heard of a "lag manager." So if I treat the shipping as an activity, a member of the team will be clearly responsible for managing it.
2. I want anything that takes time in the project to be clearly visible in the project schedule, no matter what schedule format I happen to be looking at. In a Gantt chart, each activity will be visible as a bar on the time scale, but the lags are not explicitly shown at all. In a tabular schedule, each activity will be visible as a row of information in the table, but again, the lags do not show up at all. In fact, the only place where the lag is explicitly visible is the number on the precedence arrow in the network diagram as illustrated in Figure B.1a. Why, you may ask, do I want things that take time to be visible in the schedule? Remember that, in general, the effective management of the time dimension of project performance is the key to achieving success with respect to quality and cost as well. More specifically, suppose the activities shown in Figure B.1 are on the path that is

driving the duration of my project, and also suppose I need to shorten the project duration to meet the deadline. If the shipping is a visible activity, I will consider it as an option for compressing the project duration. Maybe I can get a rush shipment or use a faster mode of transportation. If the shipping is captured in the schedule as an invisible lag, I probably will never realize that it could help solve my problem.

Start-to-Start with a Lag. A large architectural and engineering firm was performing an internal project to update its technology. The project involved installing about 50 computer-aided design workstations and training their architects and engineers to use the new workstations. In planning the project, the team realized that they did not need to wait until all 50 workstations had been installed before they began the training. In fact, they could begin the training as soon as the first 10 had been installed, which they estimated would take about a week (5 working days). You could capture this logic using a start-to-start relationship with a 5-day lag as shown in Figure B.2a. Notice that the precedence arrow is drawn from the left (start) side of the installation activity to the left (start) side of the training activity. The meaning is that the training activity can start 5 working days after the start of the installation activity. But does the "5" on the precedence arrow explain what is going on during those 5 days? Instead of using the start-to-start with a 5-day lag, we split the installation activity into two activities as shown in Figure B.2b. The "Install 10 Workstations" activity had a 5-day duration, and

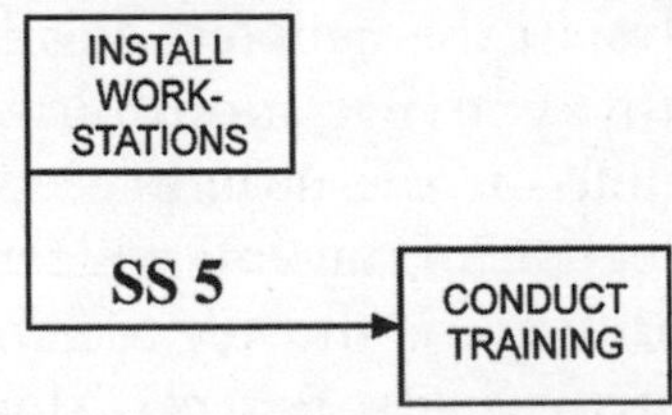

FIGURE B.2a Start-to-Start with Lag

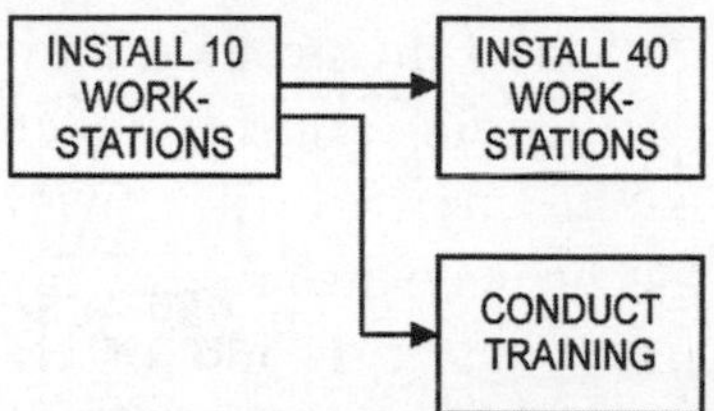

FIGURE B.2b **Predecessor Split to Eliminate Start-to-Start with Lag**

we are back to finish-to-start relationships with no lags. I will not illustrate it here, but the results of the scheduling calculations were easier to interpret with the relationship between these activities captured as in Figure B.2b than they would have been if the network had been drawn as in Figure B.2a.

Finish-to-Finish with Lag. A consulting firm was conducting a study to help its client refine its marketing strategy for a product line. The project involved collecting and analyzing a large amount of data and writing a report. The study report would be divided into two sections (simplifying here as compared to the real project). Section 1 of the report would present a statement of the problem, the objectives of the study, and a description of the methodology employed in the study. Section 2 of the report would present the results, conclusions, and recommendations. This project was extremely strategic, and the client wanted the study completed and the report delivered as quickly as possible. The project team realized that it could begin writing section 1 of the report while the data was being collected and analyzed. However, section 2 of the report could not be written (which they estimated would take 25 working days) until the data collection and analysis was complete. You could capture this logic using a finish-to-finish relationship with a 25-day lag as shown in Figure B.3a. Notice that the precedence arrow is drawn from the right (finish) side of the data collection/analysis activity to the right (finish) side of the report writing activity. The meaning is that the two activities can start independently of each other, but the report writing activity cannot finish until

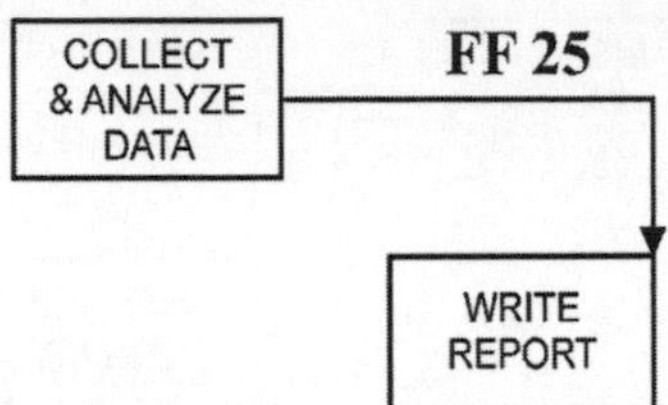

FIGURE B.3a Finish-to-Finish with Lag

25 days after the completion of the data collection/analysis activity. But does the "25" on the precedence arrow explain what is going on during those 25 days? Instead of using the finish-to-finish with a 25-day lag, we split the report writing activity into two activities as shown in Figure B.3b. The "Write Report Section 2" activity had a 25-day duration, and again, we are back to finish-to-start relationships with no lags. And again, the results of the scheduling calculations were easier to interpret with the relationship between these activities captured as in Figure B.3b than they would have been if the network had been drawn as in Figure B.3a.

Composite Relationships

A composite relationship involves two precedence arrows between the same two activities, most typically a start-to-start with lag and a finish-to-finish with lag. (Some project management software tools will not allow more than one precedence relationship

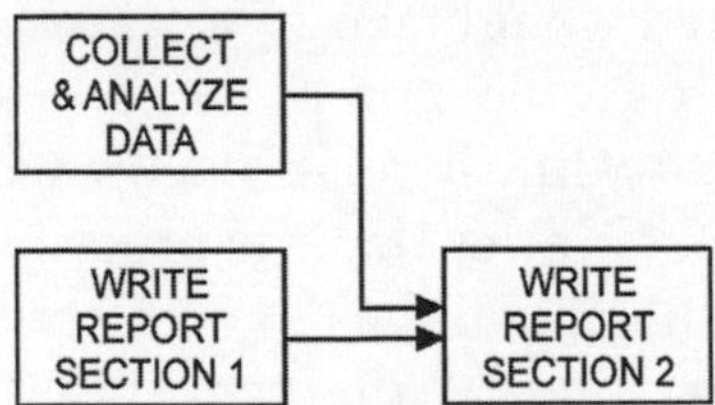

FIGURE B.3b Successor Split to Eliminate Finish-to-Finish with Lag

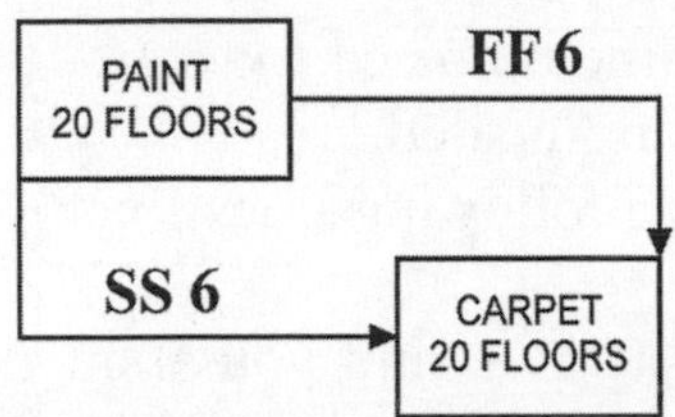

FIGURE B.4a Composite Relationship

between the same two activities, but there is a way to get around that restriction.) A hotel chain was renovating a 20-story hotel. Again, simplifying a bit for the sake of the example, the plan was to start on the 20th floor and work down, painting and carpeting each floor. The plan was to allow the painters to complete their work on each floor before the carpet installers began working on that floor. The painting and the carpeting activities were staffed so that they would each take 6 days per floor. The hotel would continue to operate while the renovation project was underway, so floors would have to be taken out of service and placed back in service as the work progressed. If you constructed the network diagram using only finish-to-start precedence relationships with no lags, it would look like Figure B.4b. This would involve forty activities: a painting activity and a carpeting activity for each floor. It was tempting to reduce the number of activities from forty to only two by using the composite relationship shown in Figure B.4a. The 6-day lag on the start-to-start relationship is the time required to paint the 20th floor before the carpet installation can begin. The 6-day lag on the finish-to-finish

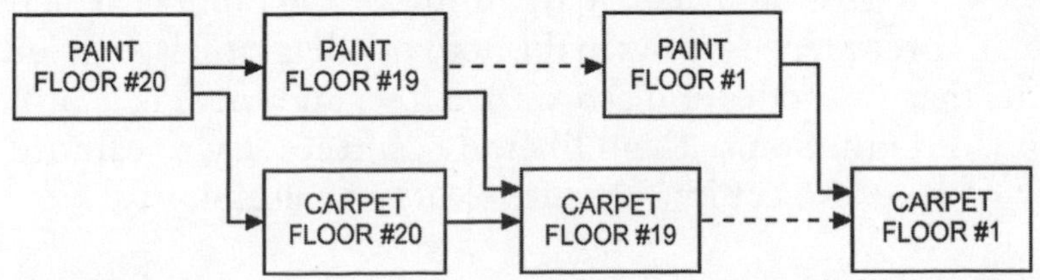

FIGURE B.4b Only Finish-to-Start Relationships with No Lags

relationship is the time required to carpet the 1st floor after all the painting has been finished.

But consider the following questions:

- As project manager, would you want the project management system to be able to tell you when the painting activity is scheduled begin on a certain floor? If the project manager doesn't care, the hotel manager would certainly care, since he or she would need to know when to take each floor out of service.
- Would you want the project management system to be able to tell you when the carpeting activity is scheduled to finish on a given floor?
- Would you want the project management system to be able to tell on which floor the painters or the carpet installers should be working on a given date?

The answers to each of the above questions should be an emphatic "Yes!" If you constructed the network as shown in Figure B.4b, the system could easily answer all of the questions. If you constructed the network using the composite relationship as shown in Figure B.4a, the system could not answer any of the questions. The only things the system could tell you are (a) when you expect to start painting the 20th floor and finish painting the 1st floor, and (b) when you expect to start carpeting the 20th floor and finish carpeting the 1st floor.

Remember, the objective here is to capture the logic of the sequencing requirements in a way that helps you manage the project. There is no incentive to minimize the number of activity nodes or precedence arrows in the network diagram. I often tell my clients that the nodes and arrows are free, and there is an infinite supply of both. So use them liberally as necessary to capture the logic of your project in a simple, clear, and useful way.

APPENDIX C

Schedule Calculations

In Chapter 9, I explained and illustrated the "forward pass" schedule calculations, which is all we really need to determine the earliest possible starting time and earliest possible completion time for each activity, the project duration, and the location(s) of the critical path(s). In this appendix, I will use the same example (from Figure 9.1) to explain and illustrate the remaining calculations, including "slack." Your project management software tool will perform all these calculations every time you direct it to calculate the schedule.

Again, let me remind you that the calculations as presented here assume two things:

- Only finish-to-start precedence relationships with no lag factors are used in the network diagram.
- The only date constraints that are entered into the project management software tool are the start date of the project and the project deadline. In other words, no constraints on the start or completion dates of activities within the project are entered into the software tool.

If either or both of the above assumptions is/are not true, the calculations become more complex than explained and illustrated here, and the interpretation of the calculation results and the identification of the critical path(s) become more challenging.

The Backward Pass Calculations

In Figure 9.1, the forward pass calculations were shown. Next, we perform the "backward pass" calculations as shown in Figure C.1. These calculations will tell us the latest allowable start time (LAS) and the latest allowable completion time (LAC) for each activity, based on the requirement that we finish the project by the deadline. The LAS and LAC values are shown in the boxes at the lower left and lower right of each node.

We start by specifying the project deadline, which is shown as the latest allowable completion time of the last activity—activity K in the example. The deadline is entered into the software tool as a date, but the software will treat it internally as a working day number. In the example, the deadline (day 40) is the same as the project duration; that is, the same as the EPC for the last activity. As a default, your software tool will set the project deadline equal to the EPC of the last activity node if you do not specify a project deadline.

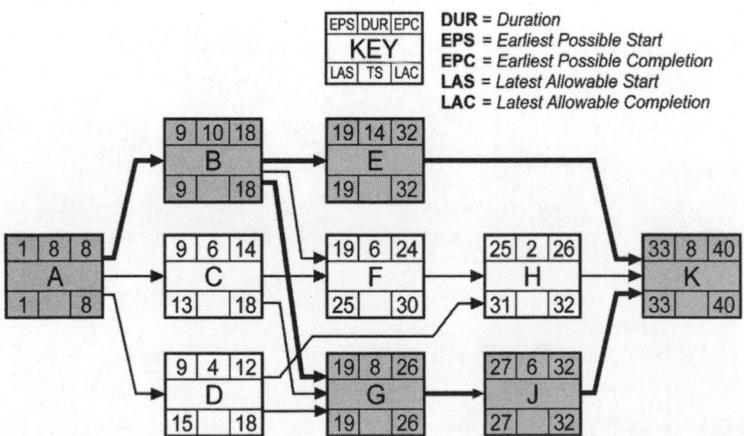

FIGURE C.1 Example of Backward Pass Schedule Calculations

Now we just reverse the logic that we used on the forward pass. If activity K must be finished on day 40 and it takes eight days to perform K, then K must be started no later than day 33.

As with the forward pass calculations, we must work in columns of activities as we proceed back through the network diagram. So we go next to activity H.

If K must start by day 33, then H must be completed by day 32. And if H has a duration of 2 working days, then it must start by day 31. Notice that we are not using the EPS and EPC values at all in making these calculations.

We apply the same logic to calculate the LAC and LAS values for activities J, E, F, and G. When we get to activity B, we encounter the first case where the activity has more than one successor. Activity B must be completed in time for E to start by 19 *and* for F to start by 25 *and* for G to start by 19. Since E and G must start earliest, they determine when B must be completed—by day 18.

This same logic applies to determining the LAC for activities C, D, and A. For example, activity D must be completed in time for G to start by 19 and for H to start by 31. Since G must start earlier than H, activity D must finish by 18.

Notice how important it is for the precedence arrows to be unambiguous. Remember that if we had used splitting and merging arrows to draw the network diagram, the arrows would be ambiguous, and the calculations would probably be incorrect.

The LAS for activity A turns out to be day 1, which is exactly what we should have expected. The forward pass calculations showed that the project has a duration of 40 working days. So if we need to finish the project by day 40, we must get it started by day 1. It is not true in general that the EPS and the LAS for the first activity will be equal. What is true in general is that the difference in working days between the EPS and the LAS of the first activity node should be equal to the difference between the EPC and the LAC of the last activity node. So if the LAC for activity K had been set at 45, then the LAS for activity A would have been 6. That means that you could wait five days (from day 1) to start the project and still finish it on day 45. Similarly, if the LAC for K had been set at 36, then the LAS for activity A would have been minus 4. You might ask, "Minus 4? What in the world does a negative number mean?" It's just a date on the project calendar that is four days earlier than day 1. So there is nothing illogical about negative numbers on the backward pass calculations. It happens whenever the project deadline is earlier than the earliest possible completion time for the project. Of course, your project management software tool will show dates for the LAS and LAC values rather than working day numbers, so you will never see negative LAS or LAV values.

Calculating and Interpreting Slack

Two types of slack—"total slack" and "free slack"—are calculated for each activity. They are defined differently and calculated differently. Most important, they are used differently in managing the project. I have noticed that people often refer to "slack" without specifying which type of slack they are talking about. In most cases, they are referring to total slack, or else they don't really know what they are talking about. Lots of people have only a very vague concept of slack.

Total slack (TS) is the amount of time that the activity can be delayed beyond its earliest possible completion time (EPC) without causing the project to run beyond the project deadline (that is, without causing the EPC of the last activity node to exceed the LAC of that node).

Take a look at activity C in Figure C.1. You could delay C by 4 days beyond its EPC value of 14 without causing the project to run beyond day 40. How do I know? I know because I have already calculated the latest time that you can finish activity C and still finish the project by the deadline—it is the LAC value of 18. So, total slack is calculated for each activity by subtracting its EPC from its LAC. The TS value can be negative, indicating that

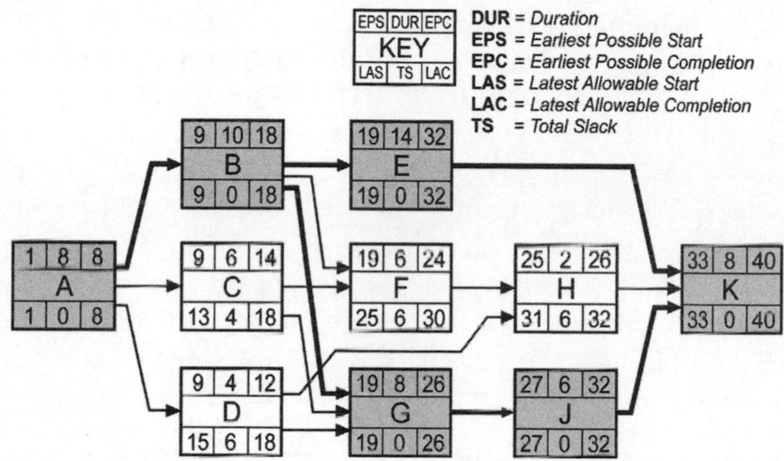

FIGURE C.2 **Example of Total Slack Calculations**

the activity is on a path that already drives the project completion date beyond the deadline.

Figure C.2 shows the example project network diagram with the total slack values in the center bottom box within each activity node.

Even though we calculate TS for each activity, we should never think of TS as "belonging to" the activity or to the team member responsible for managing the activity. Instead, think of TS as a measure of how close the activity is to being on a critical path.

Look at activity C again. Activity C is on a path that branches off the critical path following activity A and merges back into the critical path at the start of activity G. Parallel to C, the critical path runs through activity B. The total slack value of 4 for C is telling you that if you compress the critical path parallel to C (that is, if you compress activity B) by 4 days or more, *or* if you add 4 days or more to C (all else being equal), activity C will be on a critical path, specifically the path A-C-G-J-K.

Now that I have explained that concept, I need to warn you about a danger associated with total slack information in the hands of people who don't understand it (or who choose not to

Activity	Activity Manager	Estimated Duration	EPC	EPC	LAS	LAC	Total Slack
A	—	8	1	8	1	8	0
B	—	10	9	18	9	18	0
C	—	6	9	14	13	18	4
D	—	4	9	12	15	18	6
E	—	14	19	32	19	32	0
F	Frank	6	19	24	25	30	6
G	—	8	19	26	19	26	0
H	Helen	2	25	26	31	32	6
J	—	6	27	32	27	32	0
K	—	8	33	40	33	40	0

FIGURE C.3 Tabular Schedule for Example in Figure C.2

understand it). Imagine that activities F and H are managed by two different team members. Frank manages activity F, and Helen manages activity H. Now suppose we generate a tabular schedule like Figure C.3. Of course the EPC, EPS, LAS, and LAC values would appear as dates.

Frank and Helen will find their respective activities in the schedule. Each of them will probably check to be sure we spelled his or her name correctly and that we used the estimated duration they specified. Then they will immediately look in the last column to see how much slack they have, and they both see a "6." Now how do you suppose they will interpret the 6? Unless we are very lucky, both Frank and Helen will think, "I have 6 extra days." Now suppose they both take 6 extra days to get their activities done. If F starts at on day 19 and takes 12 days, it will end on day 30. So H will start on day 31. If H takes 8 days, it will end on day 38. So K will start on day 39 and end on day 46. That's six days late! What happened? Both activities had 6 days of total slack, and we only used 6 extra days on each activity, so why did we end up 6 days late? It's the same 6 days, and when Frank used it up on F, there was no slack left for H. If you recalculated the schedule after F finished on day 30, you would see that the total slack value for H would have become zero, and H would be on a new critical path driving the start of K.

What the TS values of 6 on F and H are really telling us is that F and H are on a *path* that is 6 days from being critical. The path branches off the critical path following B and merges back into the critical path at the start of K. That path (F-H) has a total duration of 8 days. Parallel to F-H, the critical path (G-J) has a total duration of 14 days. Therefore, if you add 6 or more days to F-H or you compress G-J by 6 days or more, F-H will be on a new critical path, specifically the path A-B-F-H-K.

So again, the 6 days of total slack do not "belong" to Frank or Helen or to activities F or H. Rather, the 6 days are associated with the path F-H, and they belong to the project team. No individual activity manager has the right to decide to spend the 6 days.

Because of this tendency to misinterpret and to abuse total slack, I would *never ever* distribute a schedule like the one in Figure C.3. In fact, I would never distribute a schedule that shows LAS, LAC, or TS values. These values are useful in planning the project, but published schedules should show only scheduled start and completion dates (typically the EPS and EPC) for each activity.

Free slack is a more conservative measure of scheduling flexibility. Specifically, free slack is the amount of time that the activity can be delayed beyond its earliest possible completion time (EPC) without delaying the start of any other activity beyond its earliest possible starting time (EPS). The free slack values are not shown in Figure C.2. Notice, however, that activity H can be delayed 6 days (so that it finishes on day 32) without delaying the start of its only successor, activity K. Activity C can be delayed 4 days without delaying the start of either of its successors (F and G). And activity D can be delayed 6 days without affecting the start of either of its successors (G and H). Activities that are on critical path(s) always have zero free slack. Notice that activity F also has zero free slack, because if it is delayed at all, it will delay the start of H. Although total slack values can be negative, free slack values cannot be less than zero. Free slack is used mainly to adjust project schedules to resolve temporary resource overload situations.

Critical Activities versus Critical Paths

All activities that are on any critical path are called "critical activities." However, it is not necessarily true that all paths consisting entirely of critical activities are critical paths. I know that sounds strange, but let me explain.

You may have noticed something about the total slack values of the critical activities in Figure C.2. Every activity on both critical paths has zero total slack. What is true in general is that every activity on every critical path will have the lowest total slack value in the network. In the example, the lowest total slack value is zero, because the project deadline is equal to the earliest possible completion date (40) for the project. If the project deadline were day 45, all the LAS, LAC, and TS values in the entire project would increase by 5, and every critical activity would have a TS value of 5. On the other hand, if the project deadline were day 36, all the LAS, LAC, and TS values in the entire project would decrease by 4, and every critical activity would have a TS value of minus 4. Although it is true that every critical activity will have the minimum TS value, using that fact to find the critical paths can lead to an incorrect identification of the critical paths.

You may recall that in Chapter 9, I mentioned that some of the popular project management tools identify critical path(s) incorrectly in my opinion. Figure C.4 illustrates the problem. Notice that all six activities are critical and have zero total slack, but only two of the paths through the network (A-B-D-F and A-C-E-F) have total durations of 22 days and are critical paths. The path A-C-D-F consists entirely of critical activities, but it is not a critical path. The total duration of that path is only 18 days. However, if you looked at the network diagram (or "PERT

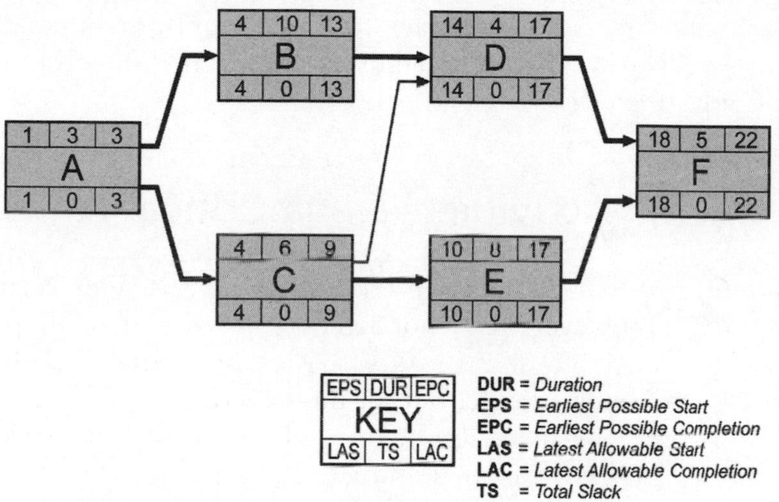

FIGURE C.4 Critical Activities versus Critical Paths

chart") produced for this project by most popular project management software tools, the arrow from activity C to activity D would be highlighted as being part of a critical path. Apparently, the software tools assume that all paths consisting entirely of activities with the minimum total slack value are critical paths. This type of error can occur only when a project has more than one critical path. Again, the error would not be fatal to a project, but it could cause confusion. Note that if you use the method of tracing back the EPS values from the end of the project to the beginning as explained and illustrated in Chapter 9, you would find the correct critical paths.

In summary, the project management software tools do a great job of performing the schedule calculations and identifying the critical activities. So when you look at a computer-generated tabular or Gantt chart schedule, the critical activities will be highlighted in some way, but it is up to you to figure out how the critical activities form critical paths.

APPENDIX D

Anticipating and Resolving Resource Overloads

In the context of project management, a **resource** is any entity that contributes to the accomplishment of project activities. Most project resources perform work and include such entities as personnel, equipment, and contractors. However, the concept of a resource (and the techniques of resource management presented in this appendix) can also be applied to entities that do not perform work, but that must be available in order for work to be performed. Examples include materials, cash, and workspace. This appendix focuses on the resource that is of greatest concern to most organizations—personnel. In a project management system, personnel resources may be identified as individuals by name or as functional groups, such as computer programmers.

The Purpose of Resource Planning

After a detailed schedule has been developed for a project, a nagging question remains to be answered: Will the resources required to execute the project according to schedule be available when needed? In the process of developing each project schedule, the average availability of resources should have been taken into consideration when activity durations were estimated as explained in Chapter 8. However, this estimating process does not guarantee that the total workload on any given resource (person or functional group) from all projects and non-project assignments will not exceed the availability of that resource during any future period. When resource overloads occur, personnel are subjected to unnecessary stress, and project activities fall behind schedule. The quality of the deliverables produced is also likely to suffer. Thus, the purpose of resource planning is to anticipate resource overloads, so that they can be resolved for the benefit of both the people and the projects. The following case illustrates the problem from the perspective of the people (human resources) who perform the activities.

Case Study: Titanium IT Solutions

Titanium IT Solutions designs and develops customized information technology for complex business requirements. Customers require total project success; that is, projects completed in accordance with specifications, on time, and within budget. Joy Peterson and Bill Cramer, both highly skilled systems engineers/developers with Titanium IT Solutions are carpooling home on Friday afternoon.

"What a week!" says Peterson as she merges onto the interstate highway. "I'm exhausted. In fact, I may just sleep all weekend. How was your week, Bill?"

"Just like another week in high school," replies Cramer somewhat cryptically.

"High school? How so?" asks Peterson.

"Do you remember how in high school you would have different teachers for each academic subject—one for math, another for English, another for history, another for science, and so on? And each teacher would give homework assignments, schedule tests, and set project deadlines independently. But nobody (except me) was looking at or even

* This case is fictitious. Any similarity to actual, existing companies, individuals, or projects is purely coincidental.

cared about the total workload that their combined assignments were creating for me at any given time. So I would end up on the same day with 150 pages of reading to be completed, two term papers due, and two major tests. Sometimes it just seemed impossible to do my best work and get it all done on time."

"In that respect, working at Titanium IT is just like being in high school again. Over any period of time, I am usually assigned to work on a bunch of activities in several different projects, each of which is being managed by a different project manager. Each project manager attempts to develop a feasible schedule for his or her project, but none of them can see my total planned workload across all the projects that I am assigned to work on—not to even mention my non-project 'day job,' which usually takes priority over the project work. So even though the schedule for each project may look feasible with respect to resource requirements, there are likely to be periods of time when I (or anybody else) may have way more work planned than I can possibly do. This past week was one of those times for me. In spite of working feverishly, I am behind schedule on activities in three different projects. The project managers are upset with me, but again, they don't see the big picture with respect to my workload."

"I get it, Bill," sighs Peterson. "You have just described the reason I am so exhausted this week. And to make matters worse, the project schedules change fairly often. It's as if the high school teachers keep changing the due dates for the assignments and the exams. But what can we do about it?"

With a chuckle, Cramer replies, "I hate to give away my best secrets, but I have found a solution that works reasonably well for me—at least to protect me from the situation. I just won't commit to project schedules. When I am asked whether I can perform the work according to schedule, I always just say that I will do my best, but it all

(*continued*)

depends on my total workload over which neither I nor apparently anybody else has any real control."

"How do the project managers react to that?" asks Peterson.

"As you can imagine, they don't like it one bit! They want me to stand up and salute the project schedule, but they understand the problem. After all, they face the same problem themselves. In fact, I think they are as frustrated about it as I am. So they usually don't press me too much. They sort of pretend that I have committed to the schedule, even though we both know that I really haven't."

Questions

1. Can you blame Cramer for his self-protection strategy of not committing to project schedules? What impact will his strategy have on project performance?
2. Is it reasonable to expect individual project managers to analyze and resolve resource overloads in situations where individuals work on several projects at the same time? If not, who can analyze and resolve the overloads?
3. What analytical approach would be required to identify and resolve resource overloads across multiple projects?

The Range of Approaches to Anticipating Resource Overloads

The approach taken to the challenge of anticipating specific resource overloads in specific future periods depends upon the number of simultaneous projects undertaken by the organization and the extent to which people are shared across multiple projects.

If the organization undertakes only a very small number of projects at one time *or* if each person is dedicated to work on only one or two projects at a time, a "short-cut approach" may be employed. The easiest and probably most effective short-cut approach is to:

- Give each person a copy of the newly developed project schedule showing only those activities in which that person will be involved, and
- Ask the person to check the schedule against his or her personal calendar and other work commitments (including the schedules for the few other projects in which he or she may be involved) and report any obvious conflicts.

A person may realize for the first time that, during a week which is three months in the future, she is scheduled to work on five major activities in two different projects, while preparing her operating budget request for the next fiscal year and participating in a two-day training program. Clearly, something's got to give! The key to this approach is that each person is given the opportunity and the responsibility to identify his own overloads.

However, if the organization shares resources (again, individuals or groups) across a significant number of simultaneous projects, short-cut approaches to the anticipation of resource overloads are inadequate. A "comprehensive approach" is required. To be effective, the comprehensive approach must capture the workload associated with all projects in which the personnel are involved. Fortunately, most popular project management software systems support the comprehensive approach as described in the next section.

The Comprehensive Approach to Anticipating Resource Overloads

The first step in the comprehensive approach is called "resource loading," and it occurs during the planning process for each new project. For each activity in the project schedule, the identity and quantity of each resource required to perform the activity (typically measured in staff-hours for personnel resources) is estimated and entered into the project management software system. Thus, we might estimate that an activity called "Develop Computer Code" should require about 30 staff-hours of Linda Baker's time and 120 staff-hours of effort from a group called "Computer Programmers." Since the estimates are attached to the activities, the project management software has the ability to determine when the resources will be needed, based on the scheduled start and completion dates for the activities. In other words, we now have a time-phased projection of resource requirements or workload for each resource (e.g., Linda Baker and the Computer Programmers). It is also necessary and possible to estimate and enter resource requirements for project-level work (such as project management) and non-project work (that is, the ongoing background process workload) for each resource.

The next step is performed periodically and must be centralized at the project portfolio level, rather than being performed at the project level. For each resource, the time-phased resource requirements are summed across all projects (as well as the non-project workload) within the project management software system. The resulting "resource profiles" can be displayed in graphical and/or tabular format. By comparing the total workload projection for each resource with the resource's planned availability, overloads during specific future periods become obvious.

The above description makes the process sound easier than it really is. Challenges include:

- Developing, maintaining, and consistently applying on all projects standard codes for identifying the organizational resources (individuals and/or groups).
- Developing the ability, confidence, and discipline to estimate resource requirements for all activities on all projects.
- Establishing the centralized infrastructure (such as a "project management office" or "PMO" as described in Appendix G)

that supports the accumulation and analysis of total resource requirements across all projects.

Resolving the Anticipated Resource Overloads

Once a specific resource overload has been anticipated in a specific future period, explicit action must be taken to resolve the overload. The action will involve either increasing the planned availability of the required resource and/or decreasing the planned workload during the period of the overload.

Common methods of increasing planned resource availability include the following:

- If the overload is significant and long-term, use the resource analysis as the justification for seeking approval to hire additional personnel.
- Plan to use overtime.
- Plan to employ temporary personnel to supplement the resource group.
- Offer an incentive to increase productivity during the period of the overload.
- Reschedule vacations, training, or other non-essential activities.

Common methods of decreasing workload on the resource include the following:

- Reassign project or non-project work to other people.
- Use a less labor-intensive approach to performing some of the activities.
- Contract out work.
- Cancel or delay the start of low-priority projects.
- Delay the start of selected activities. Most popular project management software systems provide algorithms usually

called "resource leveling" for selecting/suggesting activities to be delayed and how much to delay them. Typically, these algorithms will start by selecting activities in the lowest priority project that can be delayed without affecting the scheduled completion date of the project (i.e., activities with lots of slack).

If the methods listed above cannot resolve the overload, two last-choice options that are legitimate if authorized, but that should be avoided if possible, are:

- Reduction in the scope of one or more projects.
- Extension in the duration (scheduled completion date) of one or more projects.

The key to being able to resolve resource imbalances is the ability to anticipate them. Most of the methods listed above require advanced decision making and preparation in order to implement them when needed. Again, some centralized, project portfolio level function (usually a project management office) must direct the process of resolving the resource overloads.

The good news is that you are not required to anticipate and resolve resource overloads. Indeed, few organizations make any attempt to do so. The overloads will always be resolved automatically, just as they were in high school. The bad news is that if you fail to anticipate and resolve the overloads, the default solution will virtually always be the unauthorized application of one or both of the two options listed above that should be avoided; that is:

- Some of the work on some of the projects will never get done, and/or
- Some of the projects will be completed late.

And, as mentioned earlier, the quality of project work will be compromised, and the people working on the projects will experience unnecessary stress. These problems can be attributed primarily to the inadequacy of the organization's project management system.

APPENDIX E

How to Organize Project Budgets

Not all projects (even strategic projects) require comprehensive, detailed budgets. Consider for example a project for which the project customer is internal to the organization performing the project and on which virtually all of the work will be performed by existing salaried staff. It is just one more thing that the staff are being asked to do. Only a few marginal, out-of-pocket costs will be involved—for example: some travel and the purchase of a new software tool. A budget showing only those few marginal costs would probably be sufficient.

Projects that do require comprehensive, detailed budgets tend to have one or more of the following characteristics: (a) the project is being performed for an outside customer, (b) a primary objective or imperative is to earn a profit on the project or to minimize project cost, and/or (c) most of the costs incurred in the project, including labor, are considered marginal, out-of-pocket expenses. For such projects, the question is how to slice the budget pie into line items.

Several reasonable approaches to organizing project budgets are frequently used. For example, the budget can be broken down by:

- Standard cost categories (labor, materials, etc.)
- Project components or deliverables
- Project phases
- Team members responsible for managing the work

- Functional departments involved in the work
- Accounting periods

Each of the above approaches offers a useful analytical view of project costs. However, none of them is the most advantageous (and therefore the recommended) approach to organizing a project budget.

The Recommended Approach

This section presents the recommended approach to slicing the project budget pie. This approach is supported by all the popular project management software tools. The next section of this appendix will describe the major advantages of this approach.

First, all project costs are divided into the following two categories (which were introduced in Chapter 10):

1. **Activity-based costs** (or what some people call "direct costs"); that is, costs that are attributable to individual activities. Examples include labor, materials, leased special-purpose equipment, contractor fees, and travel expenses that are incurred in the performance of specific activities. If eliminating the activity also eliminates the cost from the project, then the cost is an activity-based cost.
2. **Project-based costs** (or what some people call "indirect costs"); that is, costs incurred in the performance of the project that are not attributable to the performance of specific activities. These costs are primarily project overhead, such as the cost of project management, leased general-purpose equipment (such as an office trailer or a tower crane on a construction project), and the cost (such as loan interest) of the capital invested in the project.

The activity-based costs are broken down by activity, so that each activity has its own budget. For any given activity, some of the budget items (typically materials, travel, contractor fees, etc.) are entered into the computer as fixed dollar amounts. Other budget items (especially labor) may be entered as a resource quantity or "resource loading" (for example, staff-hours of a specific type of labor), and the software applies a standard cost rate for that resource type to calculate a dollar amount.

As far as the project-based costs are concerned, most of them vary (accumulate) with project duration. For example, the longer the project duration, the higher will be the cost of managing the project. These costs are typically entered into the computer as a dollar amount per time period. Other project-based costs (usually project start-up and shut-down costs) do not vary with project duration, so they are entered as fixed dollar amounts.

Advantages of the Recommended Approach

The recommended approach to project budgeting as described in the previous section offers two major advantages to project managers.

1. Facilitates Effective Cost Control

First, consider a typical project for which the recommended budgeting approach has *not* been used—for example, a project with the budget broken down into standard cost categories (labor, materials, travel, etc.). Now suppose that the budget contains $600,000 for labor. Assuming that you track actual labor costs as the project is being executed, when and how will you know how you are doing (that is, whether you are on budget) with respect to the labor component? One of two things must happen. Either you run out of money for labor before the project is finished, or you complete the project without over-spending the budget for labor. Other than one of those two eventualities, you really have no way of knowing how you are doing with respect to labor cost. The way that the budget is organized absolutely prevents effective cost control on the project.

Now consider a project for which the budget is organized as recommended above. Again, assuming that you track actual costs as the project is being executed, you will know when each activity is completed whether that activity was completed on budget. More important, you will know for all the activities completed so far whether the project is on budget. That is, you will be able to compare the total actual cost to the total budgeted cost for the activities completed so far (as well as for the project-based costs incurred so far). You will know how much over or under budget you are at that point in the project. If the project is running over budget, you will know how much you need to reduce costs over the remainder of the project to complete the project on budget. The concepts for controlling cost versus budget are exactly the same as for controlling progress versus schedule, but it works only if you organize the project budget as recommended above.

2. Facilitates Cash Flow Analysis

Since we have the budgeted cost for each activity and we have the scheduled start and finish dates for each activity in the project schedule, the project management software tool can determine when the activity-based costs will be incurred. Some tools assume that all the costs for a given activity will be incurred at a constant rate over the scheduled duration of the activity. More sophisticated tools will allow you to attach some costs (such as materials costs) to the beginning of the activity and others (such as a contractor's fee) to the end of the activity, plus or minus a certain number of days.

Similarly for the project-based costs, the variable costs can be spread over the duration of the project at a constant rate. The project start-up costs can be attached to the start date of the project, and the shut-down costs can be attached to the scheduled project completion date. Cash inflows (such as progress payments) can also be attached to milestones in the project.

The result is a comprehensive cash flow analysis that can be viewed on a daily, weekly, monthly, quarterly, or annual basis. If several project plans have been planned using consistent cost codes and the plans reside in one database, the project management software tools can roll up the case flows across all projects to produce a consolidated cash flow analysis. This cash flow analysis capability is pretty much automatic in the software tools, but only if you organize the project budget as recommended above.

Cross-Classified Budgets

Depending on the capability of your project management software tool, you can also cross-classify your project budget on two or more dimensions. For example:

- Assuming that a specific team member has been assigned as the manager for each activity, the software tool may be able to present a budget in which the costs are broken down by team member and then by the activities for which that team member is responsible.
- Assuming that each activity is associated with a specific project component/deliverable (or phase), the software tool may be able to present a budget in which the costs are broken down by component/deliverable (or phase) and then by the activities associated with that component/deliverable (or phase).
- As an extension of the previous two examples, the software tool may be able to present a budget in which the costs are broken down by project component/deliverable, then by team member, and then by the activities associated with that team member and that component/deliverable.
- Assuming that each budgeted cost is categorized by type (labor, materials, travel, etc.), the software tool may be able to present a budget in which the costs are broken down by activity and then by cost category within the activity (or vice versa).

The ability to cross-classify the project budget depends mainly on the "coding structure" (that is, the categorizing information captured in the system about each activity and each cost type) and the budgeting functionality of the project management software tool. But again, you can cross-classify the project budget only if you organize the budget as recommended above.

APPENDIX F

Why Track Actual Costs and Resource Usage?

The importance of tracking actual costs and resource usage in projects depends upon the project situation. For some projects, tracking actuals is unnecessary or is not worth the effort required. In other cases, however, tracking actual costs and resource usage is an essential aspect of the project control function. In such cases, a system must be put in place to support the tracking process, and the collection/recording of the potentially voluminous quantity of data requires strong organizational discipline. Why then is tracking actual costs and resource usage on a project ever worth the effort required to accomplish it?

Depending upon the project/business environment, one or more of the following three reasons may underlie the mandate to track actual costs and resource usage on a project:

1. The financial accounting system and/or the managerial accounting system of the project organization may require the complete and accurate documentation of the ultimate actual cost of the project. This is especially true if the organization must report that actual cost to some outside organization(s), such as:
   a. To the Internal Revenue Service to justify tax write-offs.
   b. To an external project customer to justify project fees.

In other cases, management of the project organization may simply want the capability to measure the cost of executing a strategic initiative or the profitability of a project performed for an outside customer.

2. Having knowledge of actuals-to-date is a requirement for effective cost control while the project is ongoing. When estimated project costs are budgeted by activity and actual costs are tracked by activity, the project manager has a powerful tool to support his or her efforts to control costs on the project. At any given point in the project, the actual cost of the activities completed to date can be compared against the budgeted cost of those activities, so that the cost variance from budget is known continuously. Corrective actions can then be taken to reduce any negative (i.e., over budget) variance. In addition, the budgeted costs for the remaining activities can be added to the actual cost of the completed activities to develop a new estimate of the total project cost at completion.
3. Tracking actuals allows the organization to build a historical database that will support budgeting and resource planning on future projects. Such a database is especially valuable if the organization performs many projects that are very similar to each other.

Tracking actual costs and resource usage is not necessary for every project or in every project environment. However, when good reasons exist for tracking actuals, the necessary technical and procedural steps must be implemented to ensure that the process is executed on an accurate and timely basis.

APPENDIX G

The Project Management Office

Most companies today face the necessity of executing a continuing stream of strategic and highly complex projects. Examples of such projects include the development and introduction or implementation of new products, processes, and systems; design, construction, maintenance, or relocation of major facilities; marketing campaigns; mergers and acquisitions; and special events. Any given company may have dozens of such projects underway at all times, and success on each project is essential to achieving and maintaining competitiveness.

Each project team is typically quite diverse—consisting of people who represent different functional areas of the company, have different educational backgrounds, live and work in different nations and cultures, and may even speak different languages. The individuals who are selected to manage these projects face major challenges, especially since their primary job (such as engineering, marketing, etc.) may not involve project management as a primary requirement or skill.

To support their project managers and to increase their probability of success, many companies have created a "project management office" (or "PMO"). The purpose of this appendix is to explain the general concept, purposes, specific responsibilities, and requirements associated with an effective project management office.

Concept of the Project Management Office

A project management office is a staff function that

- Builds, maintains, and improves the project management system (project management policies and procedures, planning templates, project management software tools, standard codes for identifying resources and costs, standard report formats, etc.) in the organization, and
- Supports project managers and their teams in the effective application of sound project management processes to achieve project success.

Specifically excluded from this definition (although they may be included in other versions of the project management office concept) are the following responsibilities:

- To conduct financial or cost/benefit analyses to determine which projects will be undertaken.
- To actually manage projects, including the unilateral development of project plans and the direct control of performance. This is the responsibility of the individual appointed to manage each project working collaboratively with his or her team.
- To perform tasks in projects that are normally the responsibility of other functional groups, such as procurement, quality assurance, legal, or human resources departments.

Purposes

While recognizing that projects are managed by project managers and their teams, the overriding purpose of the project management office is help ensure the success of every project with respect to the quality, time, and cost dimensions of performance. More specifically, the purposes of the project management office are:

- To provide for ongoing ownership and responsibility for the application of project management in the organization.
- To provide a permanent home for project management expertise/knowledge, as individuals enter and leave the organization over time.
- To acquire the tools (such as project management software) required to manage projects effectively and efficiently.
- To ensure the consistent application of project chartering, planning, and control processes on all projects.
- To promote concise communication regarding projects within the organization.
- To provide computer support for the project management processes, freeing project managers to focus on building the team and managing the work.
- To organize and maintain an organizational repository of project information that has value in planning future projects.
- To conduct portfolio-level analyses (such as workload projections for specific resources or cash flow projections) across multiple projects.
- To continuously improve the project management system and the practice of project management within the organization.

Responsibilities

The responsibilities of the project management office can be divided into two groups: (1) those related to building and maintaining the project management system, and (2) those related to supporting the effective application of sound project management processes on specific projects.

Responsibilities in building, maintaining, and improving the project management system:

- Determine training needs for project managers/teams and acquire the appropriate training at the appropriate time.
- Establish and document project management policies and procedures.
- Create an approach to establish priorities across multiple projects and a methodology to apply those priorities to the project chartering, planning, and control processes.
- Analyze the requirements for project management and related software tools and acquire, implement, integrate, and maintain those tools. Evaluate new tools as they become available.
- Develop, disseminate, and promote the consistent application of standard coding structures and report formats.
- Create project planning templates (charters, work breakdown structures, precedence network diagrams, schedules, budgets, etc.).
- Collect and organize databases of actual project performance data (activity durations, resource usage, costs, quality measures, etc.).
- Perform project management process audits and take action to correct process deficiencies.

Responsibilities in supporting the effective application of sound project management processes on specific projects:

- Facilitate (and ensure proper methodology of) the project chartering and planning processes as performed by the project team.
- Facilitate (and ensure proper methodology of) the project control/updating process as performed by the project team.
- Perform data entry of project plan and actual performance information.
- Utilize the project management software tool(s) to perform analyses and generate reports as required.
- Analyze technical, policy, and resource relationships across multiple projects.

- Perform workload, cost, and cash flow roll-ups across multiple projects.

Requirements

For the project management office concept to work effectively, the following conditions must exist:

- Senior management must be committed to the disciplined and consistent application of formal project management processes to all projects.
- The project management office should report directly to an executive or an executive group at the level of project sponsorship; that is, the same level to which the project managers typically report.
- The project management office must be staffed with individuals who collectively possess the following types of knowledge, skills, and personal traits:
    - Expertise in project chartering, planning, and control methodologies
    - Expertise in using project management software tools
    - Expertise in implementing and integrating software tools
    - Familiarity with the business, technical, and political aspects of the projects performed in the organization
    - Interpersonal skills
    - Group facilitation skills
    - Analytical skills
    - Communication skills
    - Process discipline
    - Attention to detail
- The project management office must be equipped with the computing hardware and software necessary to support the function

APPENDIX H
Short Case Studies

Technology 1

Background

The Board of Directors at a multinational aerospace and industrial company had approved the migration from a legacy system to a super-minicomputer platform with a Unix operating system, supporting a relational database. The project would have a hardware and a software phase. In the hardware phase, a vendor was to develop software that would simulate the legacy system on the super-mini and allow the company to move off its leased mainframe. In the software phase, purchased and developed business applications would replace the simulated legacy system. As the project moved toward the end of its first year, the development of the software simulator was seriously behind schedule, no plan existed for the remainder of the hardware phase, and little thought had been given as to how to even do the software phase. The company faced the prospect of having to extend the lease on the mainframe and incur additional cost of $1.2 million. The CEO decided to name a new IT Director and adopt a formal project management methodology. The client enlisted PSI to provide a custom blend of Project Success training, consulting, and system development services.

Results

The project was a success, meeting its time, cost, and quality objectives. Other important outcomes included:

- The vendor delivered a working software simulator on time, for the agreed-upon price.
- The company released the mainframe and avoided the $1.2 million cost to extend the lease.
- The software phase had a defined scope and customer.
- A collaborative team was formed with members from each company and all key disciplines.
- The software migration completed on time and on budget, with all agreed-upon functionality.
- The project would serve as a model for successful migrations at the company's European and Asian operations as well as for new acquisitions.
- All of the company's key operations around the world operate on this integrated system.

Technology 2

Background

A multinational retail corporation consisting of several brands/divisions identified potential annual maintenance and operating cost reductions as well as operating efficiencies in excess of $200 million per year from developing and implementing a common computer system for operations. The project had undergone four years of software development little to show. The project had become a political "football" with operators threatening to develop or purchase their own systems due to Y2K pressures. Numerous product delivery commitments had been made to the prospective customers without the benefit of detailed planning. A

30-person IT staff was responsible for software development, pilot support, and customer relations. The client enlisted PSI to provide assistance.

Results

The project is ongoing; however, the initial release is being tested on time in multiple store locations. Other important outcomes of the PSI effort include:

- The project was reinvigorated, not abandoned.
- The teams re-scoped various releases in order to create a realistic set of deliverables and produce a series of bug-free software/infrastructure products.
- The realization of the need for, and planning of, internal marketing programs.
- The doubling of IT staff and the recruitment of operators to participate in design, testing, and rollout.
- The establishment of a senior team of sponsors to help guide and make critical decisions for the project team.
- The implementation of a project office for the entire program, which transitioned PSI expertise leading to self-sufficiency in planning and controlling the ongoing project.

Manufacturing Six Sigma: Manufacturing Process Improvement Case Study

The Challenge

Profits at the largest division of an aerospace/industrial company had failed to meet plan for the last several years. Quality problems continued to plague the division, highlighted by the loss of its supplier certification from its biggest customer. To address these cost and quality issues, the division launched a "Six Sigma" program to improve quality, increase customer satisfaction, and generate higher profits. First year objectives were set: (1) reduce the number of defects in delivered products by 60 percent; (2) regain the supplier certification pulled by the company's largest customer; and (3) break even on the investment in Six Sigma. The client engaged PSI to provide support.

Results

The project was a success, meeting its time, cost, and quality objectives. Other important outcomes included:

- The company regained its supplier certification within six months through significant improvement in delivered quality and a proven ability to hold and improve upon those gains.
- Delivered quality improved by 75 percent within twelve months.
- The company generated a net "profit" on its initial Six Sigma investment: tangible project savings less the cost of training, scrap, rework.
- A large multinational corporation, recognized as a leader in Six Sigma implementation, selected one of the company's black belt projects as a "project of the year," which resulted in a significant sales/marketing opportunity for the company.
- The Project Success planning and control techniques learned and practiced on Six Sigma project were applied to other types of projects for additional benefit.

Service Provider

The Challenge

A major utility company partnered with a software company to web-enable the utility's customer service process. The first project they initiated was over budget and failed to meet both time and quality objectives. The launch of the second project was delayed because neither company could agree on web site requirements, design, and development method. Concerned that the second project would be a repeat of the first, the utility company decided to utilize PSI Project Success training and consulting services. The client enlisted PSI to provide a custom blend of Project Success training, consulting, and system development services.

Results

The project was a success, meeting its time, cost, and quality objectives. Other important outcomes included:

- A collaborative working relationship has formed between the executives of the utility company and the service provider.
- The "high-performing" project team is positioned to deliver success on subsequent web-enablement projects.
- The service provider is achieving its profit objectives under the performance-pay structure.
- The companies are partnering on an additional project that will provide over $4 million in revenues for the service provider.

Product Development Case Study 1

Background

A product development team for an European equipment manufacturer was faced with a tremendous challenge. A competitor had just announced a technologically superior product, and to prevent a 25+ percent loss in market share, a radically redesigned model had to be introduced at a trade fair in 14 months. The team was only minimally staffed, and the normal development cycle for new products was 39 months. Several component systems requiring major upgrades were dependent on traditionally very long lead time parts with potentially unreliable suppliers. Additionally, sales were suffering due to severe quality problems throughout the product line, and the entire organization was primarily focused on quickly improving quality. Finally, the company president utilized a very centralized method of decision making and project teams normally were not delegated the authority to make decisions that would impact project performance.

Approach

The core project team including project manager had already completed the Project Success Method training. PSI provided consulting assistance in chartering, schedule development, crashing, resource planning, and periodic schedule updates/revisions. PSM training was conducted for new members after the team was fully staffed. With design help from PSI, the client was able to develop and implement a formal project management system.

Results

The new product was successfully completed and introduced at the trade fair in 14 months. The project manager's technical knowledge and planning skills were acknowledged, and he was promoted. The project team members all acquired new individual competencies and confidence that helped improve company performance. Other significant outcomes included:

- Due to the project charter, company management was fully aware of the potential project risks.
- The project schedule contained specific activities and duration for rigorous product testing preventing potential

shortcuts that would negatively impact product quality after development.

- The project manager was able to accurately estimate and obtain staffing needed to successfully complete the project. He used the project schedule to illustrate how any subsequent reductions in staff would delay completion, thus he was able to maintain staff throughout the project.
- Parts of the project schedule were used to communicate responsibility and delivery dates to key internal and external suppliers who were not able to participate in the project planning.
- Contingency plans were made to deal with potential supplier failures for critical long lead-time parts.
- Management was impressed with the team's knowledge of the project situation due to its detailed plans and was willing to delegate authority for more decision making. The project team gained a sense of empowerment that had not previously existed in the company.
- The knowledge discipline acquired in planning and controlling the project development product was used to assist in the resolution of broad quality problems that plagued the company.
- The schedule for the project was utilized as a template for future product development plans.

Product Development Case Study 2

The Challenge

The CEO of a large aerospace company committed the organization to delivering a new fuel control system for a small jet engine application in 7 months. If successful, the new system would displace a competitor's product and provide opportunity for significant increase in revenue and market share. To this point, the organization had never delivered a new system in less than 18 months. The project required driven people, strong teamwork between supplier and customer, and a proven project management method. The client enlisted PSI to provide support.

Results

- The company delivered the fuel system in 7 months.
- The system met its cost, weight, and functionality targets.
- A close working relationship developed between both supplier and customer.
- The project was a source of pride for the entire organization.
- The project became a model and a standard for all future development projects.

About the Author

Clinton M. (Clint) Padgett is the President and CEO of Project Success, Incorporated. Since joining the firm in 1994, Clint has provided consulting, training, and account management to clients in a wide range of industries, such as manufacturing, food/beverage, electric utility, and technology. His project experience covers many traditional and special applications, including product development, equipment installation/startup, facility construction/relocations, marketing, software/hardware system implementation and international sporting events for clients such as The Coca-Cola Company, Caterpillar Inc., Duke Energy, CNN, Time Warner, Southern Company, and others.

Immediately prior to joining PSI, Clint was an engineer for a Fortune 100 company. In that capacity, he assisted in the development, field-testing, and roll-out of new equipment, as well as managing and improving quality assurance for several of his company's major suppliers.

Clint is a graduate of Georgia Tech with a Bachelor of Electrical Engineering. He also holds a Master of Business Administration degree from Duke University's Fuqua School of Business. His professional associations include the Project Management Institute, the Institute of Electrical and Electronic Engineers, and the Product Development & Management Association, among others. Clint is also a frequent speaker at conventions, conferences, and group meetings on project management.

Index